EASTER

for the Church

compiled by

PAT FITTRO

STANDARD PUBLISHING™

Cincinnati, Ohio

Standard Publishing, Cincinnati, Ohio
A division of Standex International Corporation
© 1999 by Standard Publishing

ISBN 0-7847-1068-6

Contents

Update
Dolores Steger

Characters and Costumes:
ANNOUNCER, Sunday attire
HOST, robe
TWO CAMERA OPERATORS, robes (nonspeaking parts)
MESSENGER, robe (nonspeaking part)
ALLA GARUS, robe
PETER, robe
TRAVELER, robe
DISCIPLE, robe
JAMES, robe
CROWD MEMBER, robe

Time and Place: After the resurrection at an imaginary television studio in Bethlehem.

Scenery: Required—none
Optional—large sign with the words "CHANNEL J-O-Y" printed on it and placed in the background. Backdrop of trees, bushes or potted palms, plants, flowers (artificial or real) for stage left.

Props: Two cameras, handheld or on tripods (cameras may be made from boxes); small desk/table with chair behind it; piece of paper rolled as a scroll.

Setting: Stage right is set as a television studio. Host sits on chair behind table. One Camera Operator stands front stage right with back to audience and focuses camera on television studio action. Host and Camera Operator are in place when play begins. Stage left is set as a pathway. No characters are there when play begins.

Music: Tape/Choir/Organ/Piano

Scriptures are taken from the *New International Version* of the Bible.

Act I

Music: "Christ the Lord Is Risen Today." Announcer enters stage left and speaks when music ends.

ANNOUNCER: We welcome all of you to our Easter program, "Update," and hope that you enjoy it. *(Point to stage right.)* As you can see, we're here at Channel J-O-Y, Bethlehem's only television station. Some time has passed since the resurrection of Jesus. Now, of course, there were no television stations in those days, but if there were, how would they have handled coverage of that miraculous event? Use your imagination as we travel back in time to find out! Are you ready? Let's go!

(Music: "Christ the Lord Is Risen Today." Announcer exits stage left. Host speaks when music ends.)

HOST: Hello to all our viewers out there! This is Channel J-O-Y, your news, weather and sports station in Bethlehem and the only station in Judea to bring you annual coverage of the birth of Jesus on our "Memorable Moments" show. "Memorable Moments," seen right here every Friday night, covered the crucifixion and resurrection of Jesus last week and we hope all our viewers caught the show. If not, it will be rebroadcast in its entirety on Saturday! Don't miss it! The interviews with Mary Magdalene and the other women at the tomb were really terrific! All of the women saw Jesus after He rose from the dead. Now—on to the latest news. *(Pause.)* A lot of turmoil has been reported in Judea since the death of Jesus. His followers are in hiding for fear of being punished by the priests and Romans. It's been reported they're meeting secretly at night and only behind closed doors. We've also learned that a few of the priests believed in Jesus and what He said, but are afraid to admit it. One of the priests has admitted to it and he is now being shunned and ridiculed by the other religious leaders. As for the—

(Messenger, carrying scroll, enters front stage right and walks to Host, hands scroll to Host, then exits front stage right. Host continues with broadcast.)

HOST:—women who *(Stopping, opening scroll and reading it.)* Excuse me, ladies and gentlemen! *(Pauses.)* We have some late breaking news! It seems that some more sightings of Jesus, alive after His burial, have been confirmed. We'll interrupt our regular programming to bring you this update from Alla Garus, our reporter in the field. Come in, Alla!

(Music plays "Victory in Jesus." Alla Garus and second Camera Operator enter stage left along with Peter, Traveler, James, Disciple, and Crowd Member. All walk to front stage left and stand around Alla Garus. Camera Operator stands with back to audience and focuses on Alla Garus and the others. Host speaks when music stops.)

HOST: Alla! Can you hear me? Come in, Alla!

ALLA *(into camera):* I can hear you now! We had some technical difficulties, but they're cleared up now!

HOST: Good! Tell our viewers what's happening.

ALLA: Well, it seems Jesus has been sighted again, several times, and by different people, which tends to add more proof to the claim that He rose from the dead and lives!

HOST: And these people you mentioned, are they reliable witnesses? Can we believe them?

ALLA: I would say so. I have some of them here with me! Would you like to hear from them?

HOST: Of course. Channel J-O-Y isn't going to miss out on this scoop. Go ahead.

ALLA: I have with me several people who say they've seen Jesus recently, alive and well, walking the countryside and even talking to some of them. First, if I may, *(Bringing Peter toward the camera.)* I'd like to interview this gentleman right here. Your name, please, sir?

PETER: I'm Peter, Simon Peter.

ALLA: And you're one of Jesus' disciples, I believe?

PETER: Yes.

ALLA: Is it true that you've recently seen Jesus alive?

PETER: Yes.

ALLA: Tell us about it if you will.

PETER: Well, seven of us were out in a boat fishing at night. We hadn't caught a single fish, so we headed back to shore early the next morning. As we neared the shore, we saw a Man standing there. He called out, "Friends, haven't you any fish?" (John 21:5). We called back, "No," and "He said, 'Throw your net on the right side of the boat and you will find some'" (John 21:6). We did as He said and caught so many fish we had to tow them in. We looked at the Man again and that's when we realized it was Jesus. When we got back to shore, He had a fire going and He had some bread and fish. We cooked the fish and had breakfast with Him. I can't begin to tell you how wonderful it was to eat with our risen Lord.

ALLA: I can imagine. And you say there were six others with you to confirm your story?

PETER: That's true.

ALLA: I see. Well, thank you very much, Peter, for your story. *(Peter steps back; Alla pauses, then speaks.)* Now back to our studio in Bethlehem.

HOST: Alla, you said you had some people there who had sighted Jesus. I see some standing there and I'm sure our audience would like to hear from them too. See if you can talk with them.

ALLA: Right. *(Bringing Traveler forward to camera.)* I have with me now a traveler who sighted Jesus. Would you like to tell our audience about it, please?

TRAVELER: Certainly. It happened while my friend and I were walking in the country.

ALLA *(interrupting):* There were two of you?

TRAVELER: Yes.

ALLA: So you have someone to corroborate your story.

TRAVELER: Oh, yes.

ALLA: Go on, please.

TRAVELER: We were just walking along—minding our own business—when He appeared and walked with us. We were kept from recognizing Him immediately. Then our eyes were opened and we recognized Him.

ALLA: How's that?

TRAVELER: We had seen Him and heard Him preach many times before the crucifixion.

ALLA: And what did you do?

TRAVELER: My friend and I hurried back to Jerusalem to tell everyone what we had seen.

ALLA: I see.

HOST *(interrupting from studio):* Alla, ask the traveler if the people they told in Jerusalem believed the two of them.

ALLA *(to Traveler):* And when you got back to Jerusalem and told everyone what you had seen, did they believe you?

TRAVELER: Sadly, not a one did. Yet everyone knows the two of us are honest and truthful. I just can't understand why they didn't believe!

ALLA: Umm! Yes! Well, thank you for talking with us and for your information. *(Traveler steps back. Alla speaks to Host in studio.)* I have three more people here with me who saw Jesus. Do we have time to speak with them?

HOST: By all means. This news is too important to miss. We'll just cut the commercials and make them up later. Go on with the interviews.

ALLA: Fine. *(Bringing Disciple forward to camera.)* I have with me now a follower of Jesus, right? *(Disciple nods.)* And you say you saw Him on a mountain?

DISCIPLE: That's right—ten others besides myself.

ALLA: Ten?

DISCIPLE: Correct. They'll be happy to tell you about it if you like.

ALLA: Well, we won't have time for all eleven of you, so why don't you tell the story for the others.

DISCIPLE: Okay. Sure.

ALLA: Now, tell our viewers, where was this mountain?

DISCIPLE: In Galilee. It was more like a hill than a mountain. You know we don't have many really big mountains in Judea.

ALLA: Yes. *(Pause.)* And what happened?

DISCIPLE: Well—there He was! Right there on the hill! Some of us couldn't believe it was Him until He spoke, that is.

ALLA: He spoke? What did He say?

DISCIPLE: Beautiful words. I'll never forget them. He said, "All authority in heaven and on earth has been given to me. Therefore go and make disciples of all nations, baptizing them in the name of the Father and of the Son and of the Holy Spirit, and teaching them to obey everything I have commanded you. And surely I am with you always, to the very end of the age" (Matthew 28:18-20).

ALLA: I see what you mean by beautiful words.

HOST *(interrupting from studio)*: Alla! Ask the disciple what he and the others plan to do now.

ALLA *(to Disciple)*: Tell me, what are your plans, and the plans of the others, for the future?

DISCIPLE: We're going to do what Jesus told us to do, now that we know He'll be with us always.

ALLA: Well, thank you for telling us all about this and I hope you and your friends are successful in your mission. *(Pause. Disciple steps back. Alla brings James forward to the camera.)* And—now—I have with me James. Thank you for being with us, James!

JAMES: You're welcome.

HOST *(from studio):* Alla, is that James, the brother of Jesus?

ALLA *(to James):* James, tell me, are you the same James who is Jesus' brother?

JAMES: That's right.

ALLA: Good. Now, please tell the audience your story.

JAMES: I was alone when I saw Jesus. You know, I didn't believe He was the Savior, the Messiah, until He came to me. Now that I've seen Him risen from the dead, I know that He is Lord. And I'm sure He came to me just to give me proof of this.

ALLA: Since you now believe, what are your plans?

JAMES: I intend to spread the truth—tell everyone that Christ lives. Someday I would hope to be a leader of the believers in Jerusalem.

ALLA: And how will you spread the word?

JAMES: By preaching, by doing good deeds and, perhaps, by writing a book someday, a book that will last, so many generations to come will be able to read it.

ALLA: Do you think a book like yours would sell? Would it be profitable?

JAMES: Who knows? It's not the money that's important anyway. It's the message in the book that counts.

ALLA: Umm! Yes! Well, James, thanks for talking with us. I'm sure the audience benefited from what you had to say. *(Pause. James steps back. Alla speaks to Host in studio.)* I have one more person to interview. How are we doing for time?

HOST: Don't worry about the time. We can cut the rest of the news short. We don't have much of it anyway and this is more important.

ALLA: Okay. Good. *(Pause, bringing Crowd Member forward to camera.)* I have with me now one more person who has sighted Jesus after the resurrection. *(Speaking to Crowd Member.)* Welcome.

MEMBER: I'm pleased to be here on your program.

ALLA: Now, you saw Jesus when?

MEMBER: A crowd of us, all believers and followers of Jesus, were gathered in a field for a meeting.

ALLA: About how many of you were there?

MEMBER: I should say about five hundred! Yes. Five hundred would be the number.

ALLA: That many?

MEMBER: Oh, yes. Jesus had many followers.

ALLA: And what happened?

MEMBER: He appeared to us. Just appeared, alive and risen.

ALLA: And what was the crowd's reaction?

MEMBER: It only made our belief in Him stronger. He had told us He would rise from the dead and, when we saw that He had, any doubts that we might have had vanished. All of us are now convinced that Jesus is the risen Christ—the Savior.

ALLA: A remarkable story. And thank you very much for sharing it with us. *(Pause. Crowd Member steps back. Alla continues.)* That's all we have to report from here right now, folks, so I'll turn it back to your host in our studio in Bethlehem, and thanks for being with us.

(Music: "Victory in Jesus" as all actors front stage left exit stage left. Host speaks when music ends.)

HOST: Well, there you have it, ladies and gentlemen, Channel J-O-Y's update on the latest sightings of Jesus after His resurrection. Be sure to stay tuned for further late breaking news, which we'll be sure to bring you as soon as it comes in. *(Pauses.)* Now, on to the sports and weather, after a brief word from our sponsors.

(Music: "He Lives" as all characters return to stage for curtain call.)

Easter Art Gallery

V. Louise Cunningham

In this contemporary play, the Easter story is told through use of an art gallery and its visitors. To add interest, some of the people in the pictures step out of the frames when there are no visitors around. Some of the time Grandmother and the children face the congregation and pretend they are pointing to pictures.

Characters:

GRANDMOTHER
JUSTIN, boy
ASHLEY, girl
PETER
JUDAS
THOMAS
MATTHEW

JOHN
BARABBAS
JOANNA
MARY 1, mother of James
MARY 2, Mary Magdalene
MARY 3, sister of Martha

Costumes: Contemporary and Bible-times

Time: Present

Setting: Large picture frames in an art gallery
Scene 1—Grandmother and children in art gallery
Scene 2—Men step out of the picture frames
Scene 3—Grandmother and children
Scene 4—Women from New Testament step out of frames
Scene 5—Grandmother and children

Scene 1

Grandma and children are walking through an art gallery.

JUSTIN: So what is an art gallery, Grandma?
GRANDMA: It is a display of pictures or statues. The one we are visiting has pictures showing the time of Christ.
ASHLEY: I didn't know there were any cameras way back then.

JUSTIN: There weren't, Ashley. It's a picture someone painted.

GRANDMA: But we must remember that no one painted portraits in the time of Jesus. Much later, artists painted the disciples and other Bible people from descriptions from Bible times, but they didn't know what they really looked like. Do you remember what I told you?

JUSTIN: We should be quiet so we don't bother other people. And when we are finished we will go get pizza.

ASHLEY: Of course, you'd remember the pizza.

GRANDMA: The museum is set up so it seems you are walking through the life of Christ. *(Turns and faces the audience and points.)* We start here with the angel talking to Mary. Over here the angel is talking to Joseph.

ASHLEY: Grandma, look at this one. The baby Jesus is in the manger and the animals are gathered around. Look at the kittens sleeping on the hay over here.

JUSTIN: I like the one of the shepherds on the hill. They look really scared.

GRANDMA: Since it's so close to Easter, and we were late coming here today, I want to show you the last two rooms. After Easter we'll plan more time and go through the other rooms which show Jesus preaching and healing people. There's a picture called the "Last Supper" painted by Leonardo DaVinci.

JUSTIN: I've seen that one before.

ASHLEY: Our Sunday school teacher said it wasn't really true. They didn't sit around a table but reclined on couches.

GRANDMA: She is probably right.

(The three turn to look at the men in the pictures.)

JUSTIN: There's a picture of Judas. He looks like a bank robber.

GRANDMA: Did you know that it was predicted in the Old Testament that he would be paid thirty pieces of silver to betray Jesus?

JUSTIN: I don't understand how someone could walk with Jesus and not believe in Him.

GRANDMA: It is sad. Even today there are many people who know all about Jesus, have read about Him in the Bible, and yet won't believe in Him as their Savior.

ASHLEY: I like Peter's picture. He was a big man.

JUSTIN: What is this a picture of?

GRANDMA: It's outside the palace. Let's read what it says. Pilate is asking the crowd about releasing Barabbas. Barabbas was known as a notorious robber and murderer.

(Grandma and children exit.)

Scene 2

The men are in the picture frames. As each character speaks, he moves out of his picture frame.

THOMAS: Are they gone?

PETER: I can't see them anymore.

JUDAS: Good. I'm tired of always being the bad guy.

PETER: Well, you were. You betrayed Jesus.

JUDAS: I wouldn't talk; so did you.

PETER: And I have always regretted it. Jesus said I would betray Him three times and I did in the courtyard.

JUDAS: So I was sorry I betrayed Jesus. I returned the money they gave me. I thought He could always pull off a miracle.

THOMAS: We don't even want to talk to you.

PETER: I was really tired of keeping this expression on my face. Sometimes I get tired of being called the big fisherman if I think they are talking only about my physical size. I like to think that because of God working through me, many people were saved.

THOMAS: At least that is better than being known only as doubting Thomas. People tend to forget that I was willing to die with Jesus when He headed for Jerusalem to heal Lazarus. Then when I saw Jesus after the resurrection, I didn't need to physically touch Him. I knew He was my Lord and my God.

BARABBAS: What about me? I made it on the ten most wanted list. I couldn't believe it when the guards came to release me.

MATTHEW: You wouldn't have been released if the temple leaders didn't have their men stationed all around shouting to release you instead of Jesus.

BARABBAS: I'm sure I couldn't help that now, could I?

JOHN: Not really. If it wasn't you, it would have been someone else. The high priests wanted to get rid of Jesus.

BARABBAS: I don't understand what they had against Jesus. I did hear through the prison grapevine that He rode into Jerusalem on a colt and then turned the temple courtyard into mass confusion. I would like to have seen that.

JOHN: It was really strange to see Jesus so angry. He kept saying that they had turned His house of prayer into a den of robbers.

Usually Jesus had nothing but compassion as He ministered to people.

PETER: Shush, they are coming back.

(Everyone steps back into his frame and resumes his position, except Judas who doesn't get his foot and hand all the way into the frame.)

Scene 3

Grandma and the children enter the room.

ASHLEY: That's odd. I was sure I heard someone talking in here.

JUSTIN: Girls are always imagining things.

GRANDMA: We probably heard people talking in another room and because the place is so big we are hearing an echo.

ASHLEY: We saw this room before. I remember that picture of Peter.

JUSTIN: Look at the picture of Judas. I don't remember it looking so much like a 3-D picture. It looks as if he is about to step out of the picture.

ASHLEY: I don't remember it either. I guess we went through here so fast we didn't notice it.

GRANDMA: We made a wrong turn. We need to go this way to see the crucifixion and resurrection. After all, if Jesus didn't rise from the dead, He'd be just another religious leader.

JUSTIN: Wow! Another big room of pictures.

GRANDMA: As I said, there are at least three or four more rooms besides the ones we have seen.

JUSTIN *(faces audience and points):* What's this picture about?

GRANDMA *(turns to face congregation):* It says here it is a meeting of some Sanhedrin members when they had the trial of Jesus in the middle of the night.

JUSTIN: There's Peter out in the courtyard talking to a maid.

GRANDMA: That was the time when Peter denied knowing Jesus three times.

ASHLEY: I don't like that picture. Look how they are picking on Jesus and He is all bloody. One soldier is ready to put a crown of thorns on His head and another is holding a robe. I don't know how people can be so mean to other people.

JUSTIN: Pilate is washing his hands in this picture. He was a bad man.

GRANDMA: I don't know if he was bad as much as he was a weak man. He was afraid if the Jews rioted he would be in trouble with Rome. He didn't want to lose his job.

ASHLEY (*turns to front and points*): I really like this picture. Who is the man with the two boys?

GRANDMA: That's Simon. He was there for the Passover with his two boys. Remember when Jesus was going to Golgotha? He couldn't carry the big piece of wood that would finish making the cross. After Jesus fell, a soldier commanded Simon to carry the cross.

JUSTIN: Look at this picture. It is almost all black. I can see a man on the ground.

ASHLEY: He's dressed like a Roman soldier.

GRANDMA: That must be when the sky turned dark. There was an earthquake when Jesus died.

JUSTIN: Now I can see the faces of all the people around the cross. They all look scared.

ASHLEY: There's a Roman soldier holding a robe. I bet he won the robe of Jesus when they gambled for it.

(*Grandma and children exit.*)

Scene 4

Lights go off and then on. At this time the women replace the men in the pictures and step out of the frames.

MARY 1: Wasn't that little boy cute?

JOANNA: Both of the children were attractive and they were so well mannered. They didn't run around and yell like some children we have seen.

MARY 3: I was impressed with how much they knew about us. The girl, Ashley, knew it was me anointing the feet of Jesus.

JOANNA: It does get pretty complicated when there are three such important women named Mary in the Bible.

MARY 1: They also knew I was the Mary at the tomb on that glorious day they call Sunday. I will never forget that day. I couldn't see through my tears as I stumbled along going to the tomb. At first I felt relief to see the stone rolled away and then we went in and the tomb was empty except for a man dressed in a white robe. We were pretty scared. We ran out of there and didn't say anything because we were afraid. We found Peter and John and they went back with us.

MARY 2: When I got there I found two angels. They wanted to know why I was crying. I turned around and saw Jesus, but I didn't recognize Him. I thought He was the gardener. All He had to do was say my name and I knew it was Jesus.

(The women step back into the frames.)

Scene 5

Grandma and the children come back into the room.

GRANDMA: Whatever is the matter, Ashley?

ASHLEY: I can't forget the picture of Jesus on the cross. The soldiers were laughing and carrying on and to one side was John and Mary, the mother of Jesus. They looked so sad.

JUSTIN: I liked the tomb picture with the big stone they rolled to open or close it.

GRANDMA: My favorite is the picture of the empty tomb. Jesus died, but He rose from the dead.

JUSTIN: He had to die for our sins so we could have eternal life with God.

GRANDMA: That's right, Justin.

ASHLEY: I'm going to try and live for God. I want Jesus to be proud of me.

GRANDMA: You have the right idea. Our main purpose on earth is to honor and glorify God.

JUSTIN: I seem to remember that somewhere the Bible says that whatever we do in word or deed we should do it in the name of the Lord Jesus. Does that mean eating?

GRANDMA: I take it you are hungry, Justin. I am too. Let's go get that pizza.

JUSTIN: You know what, Grandma? I feel sorry for the disciples.

GRANDMA: Why?

JUSTIN: They didn't get to eat pizza.

Were You There?

Brenda W. Eustice

Characters:
JOHN THE APOSTLE
MARY OF BETHANY
MOURNERS (two or more)
JESUS
LAZARUS
JEDIDIAH, a Pharisee
PHARISEE 1
PHARISEE 2
JOSEPH OF ARIMATHEA
LEAH, wife of Levite priest
CHILD OF LEVITE PRIEST (written for a girl, but could be boy)
LEVITE PRIEST 2, Leah's husband
ANNA, Hebrew mother
RACHEL, Hebrew mother
CHILDREN (written for five, but could be more or less)
SOLDIERS (two)
CAIAPHAS
SERVANT GIRL
PETER
SOLDIERS (written for three, but could be done with one)
HIGH PRIEST'S SERVANTS (two)
PILATE
APOSTLES (written for three, but could be more or less)
LEVITE PRIEST 1 (in temple)
SERVANTS TO PILATE, may be male or female
SERVANTS (two) to Joseph of Arimathea, may be male or female
    (written for two, but may be more or less)
ANGEL
MARY MAGDALENE
CROWD (can utilize any cast members not involved in other roles at
    the same time)

(Note: If necessary, cast members can play more than one role. Use
care in assigning dual or triple roles to be sure enough time is
available to change head coverings, etc.)

Setting: Five acting areas are needed:

1. Sanctuary: Front left: All-purpose area to be used for various scenes as indicated in script; no scenery, few props.
2. Sanctuary: Front right: Garden scene (potted real or artificial plants to give outdoor look); Jesus' tomb (screens or cardboard painted mottled gray with opening in middle; cardboard "stone" to roll over opening); large "rock" (box covered with crumpled gray paper).
3. Balcony: Existing balcony can be used if it can be viewed from seating area; otherwise a balcony-like area can be constructed in far left front (three or four wooden plats, such as are used in warehouse, can be stacked together with a cover of plywood).
4. Overflow room: Used as interior room for various scenes; if none available, another side area can be utilized.
5. Lazarus's tomb: Back of church: a closet or small screened area can be used.

Music: Using congregational songs for much of the music involves the audience in the drama. Preferably, slides to project the words of the songs can be used. This eliminates the need for bright lights in the viewing area and the interruption of the flow of the drama as the congregation finds the appropriate page in a hymnal.

Sound: Preferably, wide-angle mikes can be used in the main areas, with pin mikes for soloists. If the church does not already have these, they can be rented from many music stores.

Props: Scene 2: pitcher, cups, table, chairs (should look to be of finer quality)
Scene 4: table (lesser quality), "dough"
Scene 5: palm branches for cast; can also be provided for audience
Scene 8: artificial fire (could be lamp in a low barrel or bucket)
Scene 9: table and a few chairs or stools (lesser quality)
Scene 10: basin with water
Scene 12: menorah, altar (should be at least waist high, can be a painted cardboard box)
Scene 13: wine cup
Scene 14: long wrapped object to resemble body
Scene 16: fog machine if available (can be rented from wedding supply house) otherwise white netting can be used

Were You There?

Lighting: If lighting for separate areas in the sanctuary is not already available, halogen floor or table lamps with dimmer switches work well and are fairly inexpensive. They can be turned on and off unobtrusively by cast members in the scene.

Sound Effects: Rooster crowing, thunder, pounding of nails, tearing cloth

Costumes: Plain straight garments with sashes and plainer headdresses for apostles, women, crowd, children. Pharisees, Caiaphas, Pilate, and Levite priests should have finer robes and head coverings. Very plain shorter garments with no head coverings for servants. Soldier costumes for soldiers. White gauzy costume for angel. Jesus should have plain garment and finer white one for resurrection scenes. Lazarus will need some winding cloths to wear for his entrance.

Bridge: *(Front of sanctuary. Lights up.)*

JOHN *(enters and walks to front):* Welcome. My name is John. I was one of Jesus' closest friends during His earthly ministry, one of His disciples. We watched Him do countless miracles. We listened while He taught the people about God and how much He loved them. He always told the truth. He was the Messiah, the One we had been waiting for for years and years and years, the One who was to save us and redeem us from the curse of sin. But none of us really understood what that would mean. It wasn't until later, after He had died and risen again, that we began to really understand. Then we wondered why we had not understood His words.

We were all Jews and we were under the control of the religious leaders called Pharisees. They saw to it that everyone kept the religious laws, and there were so many of those laws! Jesus pointed out that this wasn't what God had intended, and this made the Pharisees very angry. Jesus made them look like fools just by telling the truth. The Pharisees got more angry and then they got scared. What if everyone started following Jesus instead of them? Then something happened that made the Pharisees decide that they had to get rid of Jesus.

Instead of telling you, let me show you. Let's go to Bethany, where Lazarus, a friend of Jesus has died. Jesus had visited Lazarus and his two sisters, Mary and Martha, quite often. They had seen the healings and other miracles Jesus did. So when Lazarus got sick, his sisters sent for Jesus. But when He finally arrived, Lazarus had been dead for four days. Everyone wondered why Jesus hadn't come in time to heal Lazarus. And what happened then, well, you have to see it to believe it.

Scene 1

Tomb at Bethany. Front of church, lights dim. Mary, weeping, enters from sanctuary door; she is heartbroken. Other mourners follow her showing concern and sympathy. Jedidiah enters from another direction and stays in the background.

MARY *(moves to front of stage):* Lazarus, Lazarus my brother. If only Jesus had come . . . Oh, Lazarus.

(Begin intro of song "Because I Am"—Harvest, background tape by Sound Performance, 1994.)

JESUS *(enters from sanctuary door; approaches Mary):* Mary . . .

(Mary and Jesus sing song, "Because I Am" acting out words as they sing. At end of song: continue after break.)

****

(Note: A different solo/duet can be substituted here, or a congregational song such as "No One Understands Like Jesus" with the following dialogue:)

MARY *(turns as Jesus speaks):* Lord! *(Falls on her knees at His feet, weeping as she speaks.)* If You had been here, Lazarus wouldn't have died, but You didn't come, You didn't come. *(She is in an agony of grief.)*
JESUS: Where have you laid him?

(Mourner points to tomb at back of church. Light up on tomb. Jesus wipes tears from His eyes as He gazes at the tomb.)

MOURNERS *(murmur and point to Jesus):* See how He loved him.
SONG: "No One Understands Like Jesus" *(John W. Peterson, 1980, John W. Peterson Music Co. Stanzas 2, 3. Congregation/piano/organ)*

MARY: If only You had come. . . .

JESUS: Mary, Mary, didn't I tell you that if you believed you would see God's glory?

****

(Spotlight on Lazarus's tomb at the back of the church.)

JESUS *(looks toward back of church)*: Roll back the stone!!!

MARY *(jumps up, grabs Jesus' arm)*: No, Lord, what are You doing? *(Choking back sobs; this is very difficult for her to say.)* He's been . . . been dead four days now. The smell may be very bad!

(Stone is rolled away.)

JESUS: Lazarus!! Come forth!!!

MARY *(looks at Jesus in bewilderment, then at tomb. She is suddenly transfixed by what she sees at the tomb. A shadowy figure wrapped in winding cloths appears at the tomb entrance and steps out)*: Lazarus? *(Whispered.)* Lazarus? *(She takes a step and staggers, almost falling, her eyes riveted on the figure.)* LAZARUS!! *(Rushes down aisle to tomb, stops and reaches out tentatively—is it a ghost?—then crying and laughing, grabs him.)*

JESUS *(commandingly)*: Loose him, and let him go!

(Lazarus is helped up to front as wrappings are being taken off. He sits down.)

LAZARUS: What happened? *(Looks at hands.)* I'm still here! I had the strangest dream. *(Looks at Mary.)* Mother and Father were there . . . and Abraham. *(Looks at Jesus.)* Your cousin was there too. *(Looks around, realizes he's in a graveyard and has been wrapped in burial clothes; realization sinks in.)* It wasn't a dream—was it? I . . . I was really dead. *(Looks at Jesus.)* I heard You calling me. *(Looks around.)* Then I was here. *(Looks stunned; looks back at Jesus.)* You raised me . . . from the dead? *(Jumps up, falls on his knees at Jesus' feet.)* You are the Messiah, the Christ. Nothing can stand against You, not even death!

MARY *(falls to knees beside Lazarus)*: You even conquer death! Why didn't I trust You more?

JESUS *(pulls Lazarus and Mary to their feet and hugs them)*: Come. You must be hungry.

LAZARUS: I am! I feel like I haven't eaten for days!

(Entire group exits, laughing and praising God. Jedidiah has been with the mourners but stays in background. He doesn't leave with the rest, but stands looking at tomb, shaking his head in disbelief. Then pauses as if realizing the full significance of what has happened. Rushes out using different exit. Lights dim in front as Jedidiah leaves. Spotlight on tomb off after he leaves.)

Scene 2

Meeting room of Pharisees. Lights on in overflow area. Overflow room, divider opens. Pharisees are already in room, talking and drinking "wine." Joseph of Arimathea enters room.

PHARISEE 1: Well, Joseph of Arimathea. So you've decided to grace us with your presence.

JOSEPH: I was in Jerusalem and thought I should stop by.

(Jedidiah enters, out of breath.)

PHARISEE 1: Jedidiah, why are you rushing around in such a hurry?

JEDIDIAH: I've just come from Bethany—from the tomb of Lazarus!

PHARISEE 2: I heard he'd died. Very odd actually. They were such good friends of Jesus.

PHARISEE 1: It simply proves what we have been saying all along. Jesus is a fake.

JOSEPH: How are his sisters taking it?

JEDIDIAH: Much better than they were this morning.

PHARISEE 2: What do you mean?

JEDIDIAH: I mean Jesus came to the tomb, and Lazarus's sister Mary was there. She was devastated. She idolized her brother and Jesus appeared to be really upset too, and then He called for them to roll back the stone! *(Pause, takes drink directly from the pitcher.)*

PHARISEE 1 *(clearly impatient)*: And?? Did He go into the tomb?

JEDIDIAH: He didn't have to.

PHARISEE 1: What are you talking about?

JEDIDIAH: He didn't have to go in—because Lazarus came out to Him!!!

ALL: What?!?!?

PHARISEE 2: You're not making any sense! How could Lazarus come out to Him when he was dead?

JEDIDIAH: Because he wasn't dead anymore, that's how!

PHARISEE 1: Not dead? I was at his funeral. He was DEAD!

JEDIDIAH: Really? Well, he's not dead now! I was at his funeral too and he sure looked dead to me. But today, after the stone was rolled away, Jesus called for him to come out! And . . .

PHARISEE 1: And?!?!?!

JEDIDIAH: And Lazarus came out. He was alive. He may have been dead; but when Jesus said come out, he did. And he WAS ALIVE!!!

PHARISEE 2: That's madness! You are a madman!

JEDIDIAH: I'm telling you, I saw it with my own eyes. I was there. And Lazarus IS alive!!

PHARISEE 1: That's impossible.

JEDIDIAH: And now everyone is screaming about how Jesus can even raise the dead to life.

PHARISEE 2: I know they claim He's healed some people and raised people from the dead.

PHARISEE 1: Hysterical women who think they have every disease listed in the curses and rumors.

JOSEPH: He restored sight to the blind man and healed the crippled man they let down through the roof.

PHARISEE 2: But raise the dead??

JEDIDIAH: I tell you, I saw it.

PHARISEE 1: Then Lazarus wasn't really dead.

JEDIDIAH: He was in that tomb for four days. And I WAS at his funeral. He certainly acted dead.

PHARISEE 1: I don't care! It's some kind of trick. How else can you explain it?

JOSEPH: There IS the obvious explanation.

PHARISEE 2: What's that?

JOSEPH: That He is the Messiah!

PHARISEE 1: Oh, so now you're starting to believe in Him?

JOSEPH: I didn't say that.

PHARISEE 1: Well, let me tell you something! When this story spreads, a lot more of those ignorant fools are going to start following Him. And pretty soon no one will be coming to the synagogue or the temple! And we'll lose control. And if that happens, Rome is going to step in—and where will that leave us?

PHARISEE 2: But what can we do about it?

PHARISEE 1: We'll get rid of Him!

JOSEPH: Get rid . . . ? You mean . . . ?

PHARISEE 1: Yes! Kill Him!

JOSEPH: But you can't just . . .

PHARISEE 1: Listen! If Rome has to step in, who will get blamed for it? Us, that's who. So it's either Him or all of us.

JOSEPH: I can't believe this! The whole world has gone mad! *(Storms out.)*

JEDIDIAH *(intrigued):* How would you do it? The people think He's a king! Lay one finger on Him and they will riot. Then Rome will . . .

PHARISEE 1: We'll have to think. We'll have to plan . . .

(End of scene. Lights out or close divider. As lights go off in overflow area, lights up in front of church.)

Scene 3

Home of Levite priest, front of church. Woman holding child is surprised by her husband as she is leaving.

HUSBAND: Where are you going?

LEAH: Oh! Husband, I . . . I

HUSBAND: What is it?

LEAH: I'm taking her to . . . to . . . *(Defiantly.)* to Jesus!

HUSBAND *(horrified):* Leah!!

LEAH: I am taking her! He can heal her.

HUSBAND: But Leah! I'm a priest in the temple. You know the Pharisees' thinking. If they find out—I could be thrown out of the synagogue!!

LEAH: I don't care.

HUSBAND: Leah, please . . . the Pharisees say He's a fake, that He heals with tricks.

LEAH: He doesn't. He's real! He speaks like no one else.

HUSBAND: How do you know this?

LEAH: I . . . I've heard Him.

HUSBAND: Leah!! *(He is astounded.)*

LEAH: Husband, please. If He could heal her—so she could walk again—run—play—I have to take her! I have to! *(Runs out down center aisle.)*

(Husband stands amazed, watching her go. Lights dim.)

SONG: "Almost Persuaded" *(Traditional. Stanza 1. Congregation/piano/organ)*

(During the song, Husband paces slowly back and forth. He is genuinely torn, not wanting to flaunt the Pharisees' rulings, but desperately desiring his daughter's healing. He looks up several times, seeking guidance from Heaven. Finally stops in attitude of prayer.)

HUSBAND *(looks up, sees wife enter from back of church, carrying child. He is afraid to ask what has happened)*: Leah?

(Leah says nothing. Puts child down.)

CHILD: Father!! Look Father!! *(Runs up aisle to father who hugs her, with look of disbelief.)*

(Leah follows more slowly, a look of wonderment on her face.)

HUSBAND: Is it possible? How can this be? *(To wife.)* It was Jesus? He truly can heal?
LEAH *(in awe)*: He touched her—that was all it took—just one touch of His hand. Husband, He really is the Christ, I think. He is the One.
HUSBAND *(gazes at daughter who is dancing about)*: The Christ . . . but we have waited so long . . . but who else could do this?

(Lights dim. All leave quietly as next scene begins.)

Scene 4

Kitchen of Hebrew home, lights up in overflow room, divider opens. Two women are working with dough; comments are made about baking without leavening. Children run in.

CHILD 1: Mother! Mother!
ANNA: What? Slow down! You know you are not to be running in the house. What is so important?
CHILD 2: Jesus is coming!
CHILD 3: He's coming into town.
CHILD 4: Can we go see Him?
CHILD 5: Me, too?
CHILD 1: Please?
ALL CHILDREN: Please?! PLEASE!!

(Mothers exchange "looks.")

Anna: Well . . . I don't know.

All Children: Please, PLEASE!!

Child 2: EVERYONE else is going. Please!!

Rachel: He is the one they call the Christ.

Anna *(self-righteously):* It is blasphemy to call Him such. The Pharisees have said . . .

Child 3: Mother, if we don't go now, we might miss Him.

Child 4: And we need to stop to get some palm branches.

Rachel: Palm branches?

Child 1: To wave. Palm branches to wave.

Rachel *(somewhat defiantly):* Yes! You can go!

All Children: Hooray, hooray! *(Take Rachel's permission as meant for all of them. Children dash out.)*

Anna: Rachel, is this wise? The Pharisees . . . they are so certain He is an impostor. What if . . .

Rachel *(interrupting):* My sister, Leah—you know her—her youngest daughter had the fever. She was left with a twisted leg.

Anna: Yes, I know; it was very sad.

Rachel: She took her to Jesus, and He healed her—with just the touch of His hand, my sister said. He just touched her, and now her leg is as straight and strong as the other one. I don't care what the Pharisees say! When have they ever healed anyone? Or done anything but watch us like hawks to see if any of us is breaking one of their endless laws!

Anna *(horrified):* Rachel, such talk is blasphemy!

Rachel: I don't care. It's true! But this Man, this Jesus . . . He heals little girls . . . and, and I'm going to wave a palm branch too! *(Starts out.)*

Anna *(pausing briefly):* Wait!! Wait for me.

(Overflow room divider shut and lights off.)

Scene 5

Street in Jerusalem, lights up in front. Soldiers stroll across front, looking around.

Soldier 1: So how do you like Jerusalem so far?

SOLDIER 2: These people are mad!

SOLDIER 1: They sure are—I hope you know how to protect yourself. *(Jokingly.)*

SOLDIER 2: Maybe you'd like a demonstration. *(Joking, draws sword as does other soldier—mock sword fight with lots of noise and yelling.)*

SOLDIER 1: I guess you'll do.

SOLDIER 2: Yeah!! Bring on the madmen!!

(Crowd enters, two and three people at a time, laughing and shouting at each other to hurry. Rachel, Anna, and Children enter and join crowd in front of church, waving palm branches and shouting, "Hosanna.")

SONG: "Alleluia, He Is Coming" *(Copyright 1979, Martha Butler, Mercy Vineyard Publishing. Stanza 1, sung twice. Congregation/piano/organ.)*

(During last chorus, Jesus enters from left: walks across front slowly and out other side. Crowd is between Jesus and audience. Balcony lights go on as Jesus enters. Crowd is cheering and waving. Pharisees watch procession, from balcony, in disgust. Stir of surprise as Caiaphas enters balcony.)

CAIAPHAS *(watches a moment, then points to Jesus)*: He must die. *(Points at one of the Pharisees.)* Arrange it.

(Caiaphas leaves, others follow, except Joseph of Arimathea. Joseph continues watching Jesus. One of the Pharisees calls to him from offstage.)

PHARISEE *(offstage)*: Joseph, are you coming?

(Joseph turns reluctantly and a small palm branch can be seen in his hand. He gives a hidden wave with it, then lays it down and exits. Then Soldiers 1 and 2 enter and chase people away; pushing servant girl down as they do so. This is a game to them; they don't see the Jews as being real people. Crowd disperses, except for Rachel and Anna.)

Scene 6

RACHEL: Oh, look!! That girl is hurt!

ANNA: Rachel, come on! She's just a servant girl and the soldiers might come back.

RACHEL: No, no, we have to help her. *(Starts toward front.)*

ANNA: Rachel! *(Pauses, realizes she is going on. Exasperation.)* O-o-o-h!! *(Runs up to help, all the while looking around for the soldiers.)*

RACHEL *(reaches fallen girl)*: Are you all right? *(Helps her up.)*

SERVANT GIRL: I . . . I think so . . . oh, you shouldn't be helping me.

ANNA: Very well. *(Starts to move away.)*

RACHEL *(grabs Anna's arm as she also brushes off girl's dress)*: And why shouldn't we help you?

SERVANT GIRL: I . . . I'm a Samaritan.

(Anna utters a choking sound.)

RACHEL: Jesus told a story about the good Samaritan.

ANNA: I remember your telling me. *(It suddenly hits her that this man Jesus is truly sent from God. She steps closer to the girl and speaks kindly.)* Let us help you home.

(This scene can be altered slightly to eliminate duet; congregational song can be substituted. Dialogue as they walk slowly across front.)

SERVANT GIRL: Do you think He is the One who is to come? The Messiah?

RACHEL: Yes. I do. No one speaks as He does.

ANNA: I know what you mean. He makes God seem real.

RACHEL: He said we should love others, do to them as we'd like them to do to us.

ANNA: So many things that are so different from what the Pharisees teach.

SERVANT GIRL: I was afraid of God.

ANNA: Me too. I thought He was just waiting for us to break one of the Pharisees' rules!

RACHEL: But now that I know God loves me—everything is different. My life is different.

SERVANT GIRL: Mine too. He has given me so much.

ANNA: Me too. And I feel like I just want to thank Him for everything He's given me.

SONG: "Oh, How He Loves You and Me" *(Kurt Kaiser, 1975, Word Music. Stanza 1, sung twice. Duet-piano/organ. Or "Joyful, Joyful We Adore Thee" —traditional—stanza 1, 2, congregation/piano/organ. Exit slowly to right as song ends.)*

Bridge: *(Front of church. Lights dim.)*

JOHN *(enters from left as servant exits right):* Those women probably knew more about what Jesus was really about than we did right then. We were beginning to understand that He is the Messiah, but we still didn't understand what that really meant—for Him or for us. We didn't understand how much He loved us. We didn't understand what that love would ask Him to do. We had one last meal together—a celebration of the Passover. Then we went to a garden where Jesus liked to pray. We knew He was troubled, but we didn't know why.

(Lights dim. John fades back to enter with Jesus and Peter.)

Scene 7

Mount of Olives. Front of church. A large rock is to the right of center. Jesus, Peter and John enter from left side door.

JESUS: You will all fall away, for so it is written.
PETER *(shocked):* Not I, Lord! Even if all fall away, I won't!
JESUS: Peter, tonight, before the cock crows twice, you will have denied Me three times.
PETER: No! Not even if I die will I deny You!
JOHN: Neither will I!
JESUS: My soul is overwhelmed with sorrow. Stay here and keep watch while I pray.

(Jesus continues farther on and kneels next to rock.)

PETER: The Master is disturbed. I have never seen Him so.
JOHN: I haven't either. Did you understand what He meant at the Passover tonight . . . about giving His body for us?
PETER: Not really—I understood some of what He was trying to say. When He passed the wine, He used the cup reserved for the Messiah to come. He truly IS the Messiah. But I don't understand what He was talking about—that we would all fall away.
JOHN: As if we ever could do that. *(They both settle more comfortably and fall asleep.)*
JESUS *(returns):* Couldn't you watch with me one hour? Sleep then;

you'll need your strength for what is to come. (*Returns to rock where He has been praying.*)

SONG: "Alleluia, He Is Coming" (*stanza 2, congregation/piano/organ*)

(*Jesus returns to find them asleep again.*)

JESUS: Are you still sleeping? Enough!! The hour has come.

(*Peter and John struggle to their feet as Jesus is speaking.*)

PETER (*looking to side*): Who is coming?
JOHN: It looks like Judas. Are those soldiers with him?

(*Lights slowly fade and out. Jesus and Peter exit unobtrusively; John stays for bridge.*)

Bridge: (*Front of church on left, lights up dim.*)

JOHN: It was the beginning of the most horrible time of our lives. Jesus was arrested and dragged off to the high priest's house. We tried to put up a fight, but when they began dragging Jesus off, well, we all ran away. We were so afraid that the soldiers would be coming for us too. We all hid—all except Peter. He went sneaking back to find out where they had taken Jesus, and he followed them to the high priest's house.

(*During bridge, rock is moved farther to right. "Fire" is moved to center front.*)

Scene 8

High priest's courtyard. Front of church, lights half up. Soldier 2 is sitting next to fire with a "crown" that he is weaving.

SOLDIER 1 (*enters and approaches*): Hey! What are you doing?
SOLDIER 2: I'm making a crown.
SOLDIER 1: A crown? What is this stuff? Thorns?
SOLDIER 2: Yeah. That guy we brought in is supposed to be the Jews' "king." So I thought I would make Him a crown.

(Both soldiers laugh.)

SOLDIER 1: Hey, here comes the captain! Let's get out of here. Bring the crown, we'll see if it fits. *(Both leave laughing.)*

(Lights dim after young soldiers leave. Captain enters from left, warms hands. Servant girls enter and join soldier. All are talking, joking, laughing; tone is unrefined, crude. Peter enters quietly, somewhat stealthily, and joins group. Tries not to draw attention to himself, but others eventually notice him.)

SERVANT GIRL 1 *(to Peter):* You were with the Nazarene, Jesus.
PETER: I don't know what you are talking about! *(Moves away.)*
SERVANT GIRL 2 *(to others standing nearby):* He is one of them.
PETER: I'm not one of His!
CAPTAIN: You must be one of His followers. Your accent gives you away!
PETER *(very angry):* I don't even know this Man you are talking about!

(Rooster crows. Realization dawns on Peter and he is horrified. Just then, Jesus is led through by soldiers; He looks at Peter as He passes him. Peter, devastated, stumbles out crying. Note: If only one soldier is used, he will exit quietly after he says his line to enable him to reenter with Jesus. Front lights down, "fire" off and removed during overflow room scene.)

Scene 9

Apostles' room. As this scene is being played out, cast constituting the crowd gathers quietly under balcony in readiness for Scene 10. Lights up in overflow area. Overflow room, divider open. Apostles huddle together; attitude of fright, despair. Peter enters, still overcome with remorse.

APOSTLE 1: What happened? Where did they take Him?
APOSTLE 2: Is He still in custody? Is He at the high priest's house?
JOHN: What are they going to do to Him? Are they taking Him to Pilate?
PETER *(barely hears what they are saying; all he can do is sob, over and over):* I said I didn't even know who He was. Don't you understand? I said I didn't even know Him!!

(Overflow room, divider closed.)

Scene 10

Pilate's house. Front lights and balcony lights on. Pilate on balcony. Angry crowd below.

PILATE: I find no fault with this man Jesus.
CROWD *(angry, shouting):* Crucify Him!
PILATE: Bring me a basin!

(Servant enters with basin of water.)

PILATE *(washes his hands):* There! His blood is on you! Crucify Him if it will make you happy.

(Crowd cheers. Lights dim to almost out. Crowd quietly exits.)

Scene 11

Entire church is in darkness. Sound of nails (tape). Song: "Alleluia, He Is Coming," stanza 3. Congregation/piano/organ.

Scene 12

Interior room, Jerusalem temple. Front of church, lights up. Altar with menorah, curtain behind. Two priests enter from left; one in attitude of reverence Priest 2, (the Husband from Scene 3), the other indifferent, yawning Priest 1.

PRIEST 1: Well, I guess we're missing all the excitement.
PRIEST 2: They are really crucifying Him?
PRIEST 1: Yeah . . . about time too. All He did was stir up trouble, pretending to be the Messiah! I mean, who did He think would really believe all that stuff??
PRIEST 2: My . . . uh . . . I know a child . . . a little girl. She had a withered leg. But Jesus healed her and now she can run and play like all the other children. So . . .
PRIEST 1: So? What are you saying? That you believe Him?
PRIEST 2: I'm thinking maybe you ought to ask that little girl if He is who He said He is.

(Sound of thunder [tape]: sound of tearing cloth [tape]—curtain jerks open slightly.)

PRIEST 1 *(terrified):* Look!! Look!! The curtain to the Holy of Holies! It's torn clear in half!

(Priest 2 moves closer in wonder.)

PRIEST 1: Don't touch it! Don't even get close! You'll die! *(In horror.)* Do you think we'll get blamed for this? I'm getting out of . . . uh . . . I'm going to go find someone! *(Runs down center aisle and out.)*

PRIEST 2 *(moves closer and looks at the curtain):* I wonder. I wonder what this means. It's almost as if God is trying to tell us something.

(Lights down, Priest leaves quietly during Bridge.)

Bridge: *(Front, left. Light up on John as he enters from left.)*

JOHN: God was trying to tell us something—not that any of us understood then—or even paid much attention. All we knew was that our beloved Master, our Lord, our Friend, was in the hands of the despised Pharisees—and that they had killed Him in the most humiliating, brutal way possible. We didn't know then that His shed blood had paid the price of sin for each of us. We just knew He was dead and we were alone.

(Lights off.)

Scene 13

Pilate's home. Balcony light on. Pilate is seated in a chair, drinking cup of "wine." Servants enter, bow.

PILATE *(very irritated):* What!!!

SERVANT: My lord, there is one of the Hebrews to see you.

PILATE: A curse on those stupid people! My wife has been nagging me like the worst of shrews because I let them crucify their "King." *(Servant stands waiting.)* Oh, send him in.

JOSEPH OF ARMIATHEA *(enters, bows):* Sir, I would take the body of the

One called Jesus the Christ to *(Stops, clears throat several times; he is having a hard time dealing with this.)* to bury Him.

PILATE: What? He's dead already?

JOSEPH: He has given up the ghost, Excellency.

PILATE *(turns away, looks out window)*: He died quickly. *(Turns back.)* Yes, yes. Take Him. *(Joseph bows, leaves.)* Now that He is dead, maybe things will get back to normal.

Scene 14

Graveyard. Front, far right; lights up dim. Tomb with large round "stone" next to opening. Joseph of Arimathea enters, with Servants carrying "body" of Jesus; body is laid in tomb. Joseph pauses at entrance, head bowed. Servants hesitate by stone.

SERVANT 1: Master?

JOSEPH: Go! Wait near the wall . . . I will call you. *(Servants leave. Joseph stands looking down at Jesus in anguish.)* I couldn't have saved You! I couldn't have saved You!! Even if I had told everyone that I believed in You, I couldn't have saved You. I did everything I could. *(He is trying to convince himself.)* I wish I had told You. *(He is overcome for a moment.)* You raised Lazarus from the dead, but now . . . there isn't anyone to raise You. *(Looks up, he is crying out to God.)* Why isn't there anyone to raise Him? He said He was Your Son! Why isn't there anyone to raise Him? *(Falls to knees, then, brokenly.)* Why isn't there anyone to raise Him?

(Servants return.)

SERVANT 1: Master? The watch said it is near to sundown. We must hurry. We are more than a Sabbath journey away from home.

JOSEPH *(wearily)*: Yes. We mustn't break the Sabbath laws. *(Slowly gets to feet. Sighs.)* That's all we have left, now. *(Leaves tomb then stops and looks back.)* Roll the stone.

(Joseph leaves. Servants roll stone over tomb entrance, then follow. Front lights dim. Soldiers enter and stroll across front during dialogue.)

SOLDIER 1 *(carrying robe and thorns)*: I can't believe I won this robe!

(Soldier 2 doesn't answer; he is visibly upset.)

SOLDIER 1: Hey, don't feel so bad! Here, you can have the King's crown! *(Shoves the crown into his hand.)*
SOLDIER 2 *(throws crown down):* I don't want it! I don't want anything! *(Runs out.)*
SOLDIER 1: Well! Wonder what got into him? *(Shrugs, strolls out, trying on robe.)*

Scene 15

Apostles' room. Lights up in overflow. Overflow room, divider open. Apostles are huddled together; attitude of fear, dejection. John enters wearily.

APOSTLE 1: John. Were you there? Were you there when they *(Pause.)* crucified Him?

(John doesn't answer—walks to "window" toward audience, and looks out, attitude one of despair.)

SONG: "Were You There?" *(Traditional spiritual, stanza 1. Solo with saxophone accompaniment. They should be offstage. During song, freeze position. Lights on.)*

APOSTLE 2: Were you there? Were you there when they nailed Him to the cross?

SONG: "Were You There?" *(stanza 2)*

APOSTLE 3: Were you there? Were you there when they laid Him in the tomb?

SONG: "Were You There?" *(stanza 3)*

JOHN *(enraged):* Yes! Yes! I was there! I was the only one of His "friends" who was there! And it was horrible, Okay? Are you satisfied now?

(Peter is present but doesn't speak—attitude is one of extreme depression, remorse. Overflow room, lights off; divider stays open.)

Scene 16

Jesus' tomb. Front of church, lights dim. Tape of thunder. Light flash from inside tomb. Light up slowly as stone rolls back. Angel appears and sits on rock near entrance. Mary Magdalene comes up to tomb. Sees angel sitting on stone.

ANGEL: Whom are you seeking?

MARY *(greatly shocked):* I . . . I seek Jesus.

ANGEL: He is not here.

MARY *(alarmed):* What have you done with Him?

ANGEL: Why are you looking for the living among the dead? He is not here. He is risen!

MARY: What? I don't understand.

ANGEL: Remember what He told you? On the third day He would rise again.

MARY *(wonderingly):* Yes.

ANGEL: Go. Tell the others. *(Angel exits into tomb after Mary leaves.)*

MARY *(runs down center aisle and to the overflow room. Lights on just before she knocks, then bursts into room):* I went to the tomb! Jesus wasn't there!

APOSTLES *(shocked, speak together in a jumble):* What? Are you sure you went to the right place? Maybe you went to the wrong tomb.

MARY: No, no! It was the right tomb! The stone was rolled away.

APOSTLE 1: Impossible! That stone would take three men to move it!!

MARY: I saw an angel! He said Jesus was alive.

PETER: What? Alive?

(Peter and John exchange incredulous looks. Peter and John run out of overflow room and into sanctuary to the tomb. Angel is no longer there. They look in tomb, Peter goes inside.)

PETER *(coming out of tomb):* She was right! There's nothing there but the burial wrappings. *(They look around, incredulous.)*

JOHN: This is the right tomb, isn't it?

(They exchange looks. The possibility that what Mary Magdalene had told them was true begins to dawn on them. Expressions of incredulity, hope, excitement. Together they begin to run back to report what they found.)

PETER *(keeps up with John, then slows, meditates):* Can it be true? Can it really be true, that Jesus is alive? How could that be? Those things

He said, about rebuilding the temple in three days—could He have been talking about himself? (*Louder, with wonder.*) He could really be alive! (*Begins to run again, then almost immediately stops.*) But what difference would it make? (*Dejectedly.*) I denied Him. He will never want Me around. I denied Him. I said I didn't even know who He was. (*Continues sadly back to overflow room.*)

JOHN (*enters overflow room breathlessly to report to others*): It's as she said!! The tomb is empty!! Jesus isn't there!

APOSTLES (*all talking at once*): How could it be? Who moved the stone? How could He be alive? But remember Lazarus—he was raised from the dead.

(*Peter enters moments later. Apostles continue excited babble. As they are speaking, cloudy mist appears and Jesus steps out of it into their midst. All fall back in fear.*)

APOSTLES: It's a ghost!

(*Jesus turns to Peter, holds out His hand. Peter moves toward Him slowly as if in a daze.*)

PETER: Lord. (*Hesitantly.*) Is . . . is it really You? You're alive? You're alive? (*Reaches out and touches Him, then takes His hand, and falls to his knees sobbing.*) I'm sorry . . . I'm . . .

JESUS (*pulls Peter to his feet and hugs him, soothingly*): Peter, Peter.

PETER (*to others*): He's alive!! It's He!! He's real!! Jesus forgives me!

APOSTLES (*frozen in disbelief until Peter speaks to them, then they hesitantly move toward Jesus*): You're really here. You're really alive. (*Hesitation gives way to jubilation.*)

PETER: He's alive! He's risen . . . FROM THE DEAD!!!

(*Jubilation continues as lights slowly dim in overflow room. All lights on in sanctuary. Rest of cast gathers in sanctuary. Apostles led by Peter rush in.*)

APOSTLES: He's alive! Jesus is risen from the dead! (*Word spreads from apostles to rest of cast and to audience. Praise and jubilation.*)

JOSEPH OF ARIMATHEA (*rushes in*): What are you saying? What is happening?

PETER: He's alive!! We've seen Him!!

JOSEPH: Alive!! Jesus? But how? Who?

PETER: Who can explain how? But it's true. We all saw Him.

JOSEPH: But . . . (*Wants to believe but cannot allow himself to.*)

(*Song begins softly.*)

PETER (*lays his hand on Joseph's arm*): Joseph. Don't try to explain God's ways. Just . . . believe.

SONG: "Alleluia, He Is Coming," (*stanza 4, or "Easter Song" Latter Rain Music, Sparrow Corp., 1974. Congregation/piano/organ. Could also be solo/duet for first run-through with congregation joining in for a second.*)

(*During song, cast disperses except Peter and Joseph. They move to front, center and take off headcoverings and/or false beards. After song, continue dialogue.*)

JOSEPH (*to audience*): I played Joseph of Arimathea. He wanted to believe in Jesus but he was afraid—afraid of what others would think; afraid of how it would change his life. Have you ever felt that way? Don't ever be afraid of Jesus. He loves you more than you could ever imagine; and whatever changes may come, they will be good ones. Whatever other people think, having Jesus in your life makes it better. So, if you've not asked Jesus into your life because of fear, come to Him now. He can handle all your fears.

PETER: I played Peter. Peter didn't think Jesus could ever forgive him for denying him—it was too terrible a sin for even Jesus to forgive. Do you maybe feel that way—that you've done something "too terrible," or maybe just a lot of smaller things that all together are too much for Jesus to forgive? Don't worry. Nothing is too big or too terrible or too much for Jesus. Peter found that out when Jesus held out His hand—that all Jesus wants is to make things better. And He can do that for you, for anyone. He holds out His hand. All you have to do is reach out and take it.

(*Balcony, lights up. Cloudy mist, Jesus emerges from "cloud," holding out His hand, smiling. Bridge can be included here, such as Scripture: John 1:10-13. Cloud increases and Jesus slowly merges back into it. Sanctuary lights dim.*)

CLOSING REMARKS if desired, invitation.

SONG: "The Old Rugged Cross" (*congregation/piano/organ*)

The Risen Lord

Lillian Robbins

Characters:

JESUS

12 APOSTLES: SIMON PETER; ANDREW; JAMES; JOHN; PHILIP; BARTHOLOMEW; MATTHEW; THOMAS; JAMES, SON OF ALPHAEUS; SIMON (ZELOTES); JUDAS, JAMES'S BROTHER; JUDAS ISCARIOT

ANGEL 1

ANGEL 2

MARY, mother of James

MARY MAGDALENE

SALOME

JOANNA

OTHER WOMAN

EXTRA MEN FOR GARDEN SCENE

(Have someone announce scenes or prepare printed programs.)

Act I: Jesus' entry into Jerusalem
   Scene 1: Road to Jerusalem before triumphal entry
   Scene 2: Entering Jerusalem for Passover
Act II: Passover
   Scene 1: Upper room
   Scene 2: Garden of Gethsemane
Act III: Jesus' resurrection
   Scene 1: On road to grave sight
   Scene 2: At Jesus' tomb

Costumes: Attire for biblical characters, sandals for men, angel costumes

Props: Seating arrangements to appear as huge stones, trees (cut and placed or artificial trees or paintings), money bag for Judas, table, chairs or cushions for reclining, dishes, loaf of bread, cup of juice, sop, swords (fake), basin, pitcher of water, towel, container for spices, large scene of cave with stone rolled aside, spotlight

Act I—Scene 1

Jesus' entry into Jerusalem, on road to Jerusalem before triumphal entry. Jesus and twelve apostles enter.

PETER: I wonder what this visit to Jerusalem will bring.

ANDREW: We never know what is ahead of us. I just know I want to be with Jesus.

JAMES: We'll probably see some more miracles here.

MATTHEW: I hope we have some time alone with Jesus. There are so many more things I need to learn from Him.

JOHN (*pushes by others to get beside Jesus*): Jesus, You know I want to be near You. But You have been walking so fast.

JESUS: I know, John.

JOHN: I want to be with You always.

JESUS: I know that, too, John. (*To group.*) Men, let's stop here for a little while. (*All sit.*)

THOMAS: It hardly seems like it's time for the Passover again.

MATTHEW: But, Thomas, we've been to so many places since last year. Just think of all the multitudes who have followed us.

THOMAS: I know. Even the women want to hear Jesus speak.

ANDREW: I wonder just how many miles we have walked and how many miracles we have seen.

JAMES: I'll never forget being on that stormy sea when Jesus was asleep. Even the big fisherman was frightened.

BARTHOLOMEW: We would have surely perished if Jesus had not performed a miracle then.

PHILIP (*speaking to Judas Iscariot*): How do you feel about being in Jerusalem again, Judas?

JUDAS ISCARIOT: I expect it will be exciting. There will be many people here for the Passover.

BARTHOLOMEW: We will probably see some people we haven't seen in a long time. I think it's good sometimes to renew old acquaintances.

JAMES, SON OF ALPHAEUS: I'm sure we'll see some of the Pharisees.

JUDAS, JAMES'S BROTHER: And the chief priests and scribes and elders who continue to confront Jesus. It seems like they always want to make trouble.

SIMON: I wonder why they don't accept Jesus. Surely they can hear the word of God in the lessons Jesus teaches. And the miracles we've seen are directly from Jehovah God. The lame rise up and walk. A man blind from birth was made to see. Even the winds

The Risen Lord

and seas obey Jesus' voice. I just don't know how anybody cannot believe in Him.

PETER: Those men are just self-righteous. Their hearts are not right with God. They have real problems and just won't see it.

JOHN (to Jesus): Lord, how can men refuse to hear Your words?

JESUS: There are many who hear but don't understand, and can see but are blind. (Standing.) Men, it is time for us to enter Jerusalem. (Men stand.) Bartholomew, you and Simon go into the village. There you will find a donkey tied up. A colt will be with her. Loose them and bring them to me.

SIMON: But, Master, what will the owners say when we start to take their animals?

JESUS: Just tell them the Lord needs them. They will let you bring them to me. Now go on to the village. (To the others.) And the rest of you will follow me.

BARTHOLOMEW (as he and Simon exit): Why does Jesus want a donkey and a colt? We don't usually have animals with us where we go.

SIMON: I don't know. But I do know it's not for us to question the Master. We will just do what He says. (Exit.)

MATTHEW (as group leaves): I'm really looking forward to entering Jerusalem. I think I'll see it now as I never saw it before.

PHILIP: And we'll all be together. (All exit.)

Act I—Scene 2

On the road to Jerusalem before Passover. Jesus and apostles enter.

JOHN: Lord, You must be tired. You have spent so many hours among the people. Could we not stop here for a little rest?

JESUS: Yes, this will be a good place. (All sit.) I have a few more things to say to all of you.

MATTHEW: Master, we have so much to learn. Will You teach us more now?

JESUS: Many things you have heard of me. Some you will remember, some you will forget. But have no fear. The Lord God will provide you with knowledge and understanding.

JAMES, SON OF ALPHAEUS: Sometimes I have so many questions. Even at night while I am trying to sleep, I wonder what some of the things I've seen and heard really mean.

JESUS: I will talk to you more later. At the Passover meal, I will reveal truths that will be with you all the days of your life. The time has been short for my teaching, but you will be prepared. I will give you some very important information, even tonight.

JUDAS, JAMES'S BROTHER: Will You teach us more about the kingdom?

JESUS: First we must prepare for the Passover meal.

ANDREW: Where will we eat the Passover this time?

JESUS: A place will be provided. Peter, you and John will go and prepare the Passover meal that we may eat it together.

PETER: Lord, You haven't told us where to make the arrangements.

JESUS: As you go into the city, you will see a man carrying a pitcher of water. Follow him to the house where he enters.

JOHN: What should we say to him?

JESUS: Speak to the man of the house. Tell him the Master needs to use the guestchamber that He may eat this Passover with His disciples. He will show you a large upper room. Make preparations there.

PETER: And, Lord, when will You come there?

JESUS: You just get everything ready. We will be there when the time is right.

JOHN (*as he and Peter leave*): It is a great privilege to be chosen to prepare the Passover for the Lord. Don't you think so, Peter?

PETER: Everything we do for Him is a great privilege. Come on, John. Let's be on our way.

JESUS (*to others*): Men, you remember the command from long ago that we eat the Passover meal. You will see a meaning tonight far deeper than you ever saw before. Come, let's prepare ourselves for this last Passover we will share together.

THOMAS (*as they leave*): What does He mean, the last Passover?

JUDAS ISCARIOT: I don't know. There are many things Jesus says that I don't fully understand, but I want to hear every word anyway. (*All exit.*)

Act II—Scene 1

The Passover in the upper room. Peter and John are putting food on the table as Jesus and other apostles enter.

PETER: Jesus, we thought You would be coming soon.

JOHN: Master, all is ready for the Passover feast.

(*Jesus and men sit at table or recline on cushions on the floor.*)

JESUS: We have come here just as the men of old did. Through Moses Jehovah God commanded the children of Israel to commemorate their deliverance from death in the land of Egypt. The firstborn of every family in Egypt died that fateful night, but the Lord passed over the homes of the Israelites where the blood of the lamb was sprinkled on the lintels of the doors. Their firstborn children were saved from death.

JAMES: I can always picture that scene in my mind. What a wonderful blessing that was for our forefathers.

JESUS: The Father in Heaven wanted to be sure His people didn't forget it. That is why we celebrate the Passover even today. Our people across the land are meeting together just as we are here. We are united in our thoughts of the Father's mercy even though we are far apart from many of our friends.

(Jesus rises from table, takes towel and wraps it around His body, pours water in basin, washes each apostle's feet, dries with towel. He approaches Peter last.)

PETER: Lord, are You going to wash my feet?

JESUS: What I do now, Peter, you don't know. But you will know in time to come.

PETER: No, Lord. You shall never wash my feet.

JESUS: If I don't wash your feet, you have no part of me.

PETER: Then, Lord, not my feet only, but my hands and my head. *(Holds hands out toward Jesus.)*

(Jesus completes washing. As He moves basin of water and removes towel, He speaks.)

JESUS: I have given you an example. Listen to what I say. The servant is not greater than his lord. I am your Lord, and if I have washed your feet, you should wash one another's feet.

JESUS *(sits at table, takes bread and prays)*: Father God, we gather in Your name to remember Your saving grace in the land of Egypt long ago. We thank You for this unleavened bread, and we pray Your blessings on Your people who eat it. May it be a continual memorial throughout the ages. Amen.

(Jesus breaks bread, passes to apostles and they hold bread.)

JESUS: Take this bread and eat it. It is my body, broken for you. Do this in remembrance of me. *(All eat.)*

JESUS (*holds cup*): Father, I thank You for Your love and mercy. I pray now for those who gather to remember Your deliverance for them. Amen. (*To men.*) All of you drink from this cup. This is my blood of the new covenant. It is shed for many for the remission of sins. Drink this in remembrance of me. I will not drink again of this fruit of the vine until I drink it in my Father's kingdom.

(*Cup is passed, each man drinks, meal continues.*)

JESUS: One of you will betray me.
PETER (*speaking to John who sits beside Jesus*): Ask Him who it is.
BARTHOLOMEW: Is it I, Lord?
JUDAS, JAMES'S BROTHER: Lord, is it I?
ANDREW: Is it I?
JAMES: Lord, is it I?
JOHN: It is not I, is it, Lord?
PETER: Not I, is it, Lord?
PHILIP: Is it I?
MATTHEW: Lord, surely it is not I?
THOMAS: Is it I?
JAMES, SON OF ALPHAEUS: Not I, is it, Lord?
SIMON: Is it I, Lord?

(*Judas Iscariot dips bread in dish at same time as Jesus.*)

JESUS: He that dips with me is the one.
JUDAS ISCARIOT: Is it I, Lord?
JESUS (*puts His bread to the mouth of Judas*): You have said it. (*Judas eats.*) What you are going to do, go and do quickly.

(*Judas rushes out.*)

JESUS (*to others*): I have a new commandment for you, that you love one another. As I have loved you, you love one another. A little while I am with you, then I must go. You will seek me, but cannot find me.
JAMES, SON OF ALPHAEUS: What does He mean, a little while?
PHILIP: And He says then we can't find Him?
THOMAS: There is so much I don't understand. I wish He would make it clear.
JESUS: When I am risen, I will meet you again in Galilee.

(Jesus starts singing as He stands, others join in. Sing "Abide with Me." After song all follow Jesus offstage.)

Act II—Scene 2

Garden of Gethsemane. Jesus and all apostles except Judas Iscariot enter.

JESUS: Tonight all of you will be offended because of me. You will be scattered in all directions.

PETER: Not I, Lord. I will never leave You.

JESUS: Peter, Peter, this night before the cock crows twice, you will deny me three times.

PETER: No, Lord. I am ready to die for You. And I will never leave You.

JESUS *(to apostles in rear):* You men wait here. Sit and pray. Peter, James, and John, go with me farther into the garden. *(After a few steps, Jesus speaks to the three.)* Watch here and pray. My soul is exceedingly sorrowful. I will go on yonder. *(Goes littler farther, kneels on ground.)* Oh, my Father, I know that all things are possible with You. My heart is so very heavy. I pray that You will take away this cup of sorrow from me. Father, is there some other way? I love You, Father. I trust You. And I just pray to be delivered from this sorrow. But I submit to Your will. Not my will, but Yours be done.

JESUS *(goes back to men, awakes them from sleep):* Peter, could you not watch one hour? Watch and pray that you enter not into temptation. The spirit is willing, but the flesh is weak. *(He goes forward again, kneels and prays.)* Oh, Father, if I must drink of this bitter cup, Thy will be done. *(Remains few minutes praying silently.)*

(Jesus returns to men, finds them asleep, leaves and goes to pray again.)

JESUS *(kneels):* Oh, Father God, hear My prayer. *(Angel appears near Jesus.)* Oh, my Father, if it must be, if this cup may not be taken from me, Thy will be done. *(Prays silently. Angel touches His shoulder. After few minutes, Angel leaves. Jesus rises and looks up.)* My Father, Thy will be done. *(Jesus goes back to men.)* Sleep on now and take your rest. *(Sits and bows head in hands.)*

JESUS *(to men):* The hour is at hand when the Son of man is betrayed into the hands of sinners. Rise up, let us be going. *(As they move on, Judas and other men enter.)*

JUDAS ISCARIOT *(goes forward and kisses Jesus):* Hail, Master.

JESUS: Friend, do what you came for.

(Men come to arrest Jesus. Peter lifts his sword and seemingly cuts off right ear of one of them.)

JESUS: Put up your sword. *(He touches the ear of the soldier.)* I could pray even now and the Father would send twelve legions of angels. But how then would the Scriptures be fulfilled? This must be.

JESUS *(to soldiers)*: Are you come out as against a thief with swords and with staves to take me? I was daily with you in the temple teaching, and you took me not.

(They take Jesus away and the apostles flee in different directions. Peter hesitates, then follows slowly in the direction of Jesus' exit.)

Act III—Scene 1

Jesus' resurrection, on the road to the grave site. Women enter.

MARY: I regret that we couldn't properly prepare the body of Jesus for burial. If it had not been the approaching Sabbath, we would have had time.

MARY MAGDALENE: But now we will place these sweet-smelling spices in His tomb. The Lord will understand. He will know how much we love Him.

SALOME: I am anxious to get to the tomb. But I wonder how we will ever get that big stone rolled away from the entrance to the cave.

MARY: Perhaps there will be some of His disciples there who will do that for us.

SALOME: I suppose some of the men will come to His grave in the early morning. What about the special twelve who have been with Him everywhere?

MARY MAGDALENE: Judas Iscariot will not come. He is the one who led the soldiers to the garden where they arrested Jesus. I just don't understand how he could do that.

JOANNA: I still can't believe they would dare kill Jesus. He was such a good man.

OTHER WOMAN: They had no reason to crucify Him. He hadn't done anything wrong.

JOANNA: He just went about doing good, healing the sick and teaching a better way of life, how we should really love one another.

MARY: That was the most horrible thing I have ever seen, our Lord hanging on a cross between two criminals.

SALOME: He was so bruised from the abuse of the soldiers at the trial.

MARY: And even then they put that heavy cross on His back to carry up the hill to Calvary.

SALOME: If I had been strong enough, I would have been glad to carry it for Him.

MARY MAGDALENE: The sound of that hammer driving nails into His hands and feet rang in my ears all night.

JOANNA: And the thud when they dropped the cross in the ground sounded all across the hill.

MARY MAGDALENE: I wanted to just mop His brow with a cool cloth and give Him a drink of water.

OTHER WOMAN: Can you imagine, with His lips so parched, the soldiers offered Him vinegar to drink?

MARY MAGDALENE: I was sobbing so, I could hardly hear Him when He prayed, "Father forgive them." Oh, what a man with a heart so full of love.

SALOME: I just couldn't bear it when that soldier thrust his sword into Jesus' side.

OTHER WOMAN: And blood and water gushed forth.

MARY: No wonder the earth was dark and the earthquake shook the rocks asunder.

OTHER WOMAN: I wonder what those chief priests and elders thought then.

(A loud noise is heard offstage.)

MARY: What was that noise?

MARY MAGDALENE: It seems as if the earth is shaking under my feet.

SALOME: I feel it, too, almost like when Jesus was crucified.

JOANNA: It is so frightening! What do you think is happening?

OTHER WOMAN: An earthquake. Surely it is an earthquake.

MARY MAGDALENE: Come on, hurry, let's see what is happening.

(All exit.)

Act III—Scene 2

At the tomb. Women enter stage opposite scene of cave.

MARY MAGDALENE *(enters first, speaks back to others before they enter)*: Come on. It's there just ahead.

(Others enter as angels appear. Spotlight on angels.)

MARY: The bright light! Who? What? Look, the stone is rolled away.

SALOME *(holds on to other woman):* I'm afraid. I've never seen a man like that. Look at his face. It looks like—lightning! And his robe, it's as white as snow!

OTHER WOMAN: I don't know what to say. But this is where Jesus was buried. I know. I watched them lay Him in a tomb. There, that is the cave. *(Points.)*

ANGEL 1: Don't be afraid. I know you have come to see Jesus of Nazareth who was crucified. He is not here. He is risen, just as He said while He was still with you.

ANGEL 2: Why seek ye the living among the dead? Remember how He spoke to you when He was in Galilee? He said He would rise the third day.

MARY MAGDALENE: Arise from the grave?

MARY: Is He really alive?

ANGEL 1: Come see where He lay.

(Women follow angels offstage—return immediately.)

MARY MAGDALENE: He's alive! He's alive!

OTHER WOMAN: He's risen from the dead. Even death couldn't hold our Lord.

SALOME: Hallelujah! Jesus is alive!

JOANNA: He conquered death. He rose from the grave.

ANGEL 1: Now go quickly and tell His disciples He is risen from the grave.

ANGEL 2: Tell them they will see Jesus in Galilee. Be sure to tell Peter that Jesus is alive just as He said. He will see Jesus in Galilee.

(Women start to leave.)

MARY MAGDALENE: Praise the Lord! Jesus is alive!

MARY AND SALOME: Alive! Alive! Alive!

JOANNA: He came forth from the grave!

OTHER WOMAN: Death could not hold Him.

MARY MAGDALENE: He is victorious. Our glorious Lord is alive forevermore!

(All exit.)

The Risen Lord

The Wise Man and the Shepherd

Judy Land

Synopsis: From Luke 24. On the third day after Jesus' crucifixion, the son of one of the Magi who saw Christ as a child (Shethar)* and the nephew of one of the shepherds who saw Him as an infant (Cleopas)* meet on the road to Emmaus and discuss what has happened to their Lord. As they walk and talk, they remember scenes from the nativity and boyhood of Jesus, and discuss prophecy and fulfillment. Scenes are displayed on overhead projector or video. They are eventually met by Christ himself, and continue walking and talking with Him. In the last scene, the two appear before the eleven disciples in the room in Jerusalem, and Christ appears in their midst as described in Luke 24:33-49. Wherever possible, direct quotes from the account in Luke *(New International Version)* are used. (*Since the identity of both men on the road to Emmaus is not stated in the biblical account, other than one is named Cleopas, I have taken the liberty of giving both men a fictional past which helps to put the history of Christ's birth in perspective. *The Wycliffe Bible Commentary* says that Cleopas was possibly the husband of one of the Marys and the father of James the Less, but does not identify the other disciple.)

Characters:
JESUS
CLEOPAS
SHETHAR
ELEVEN DISCIPLES
VARIOUS MEN, WOMEN AND CHILDREN IN FAMILY GROUPS

Participants:
ADULT CHOIR
CHILDREN'S CHOIR (in costume)

Props: Slide screen or large video screen, slides (can be ordered individually from Christian Images & Slides at 1-800-451-2911), olive or juniper trees or other shrubs typical of Israel, palm branches, table and benches for the upper room

Costumes: Jewish costume from Jesus' time, fabric of plain burlap or muslin, except on Shethar, who should wear a rolled turban on his head and clothing made of different fabric in deeper colors. Shethar's belt could be cording instead of fabric.

CHOIR: "Tell Me the Story of Jesus" (*or your selection*)

Scene 1

While Choir sings, the following scene unfolds, in Christ's time, near Jerusalem. Men, women, boys and girls walk two directions along dirt path across stage. Some carry baskets, some walk with packs slung on their backs. Some are in a hurry and some walk slowly. Shethar is carrying a heavy pack. He is jostled by another, who apologizes and hurries along. Cleopas comes along and picks up something that fell from the pack.

CLEOPAS (*handing Shethar the object*): Here, you dropped this.
SHETHAR (*absently*): Oh, thank you.
CLEOPAS: Hey, I saw you yesterday. Weren't you one of the followers of Jesus?
SHETHAR (*suspiciously*): Who are you?
CLEOPAS: Don't worry. I'm a follower too, (*Looks down.*) although a disappointed one.
SHETHAR: I know. Were you there at the cross? Did you see the crucifixion?
CLEOPAS: Yes. I was there.

(*Two men stop walking but continue talking—mime—while Choir sings.*)

CHOIR: "Were You There?" (*or your selection*)
VIDEO: Scenes of crucifixion

SHETHAR (*sighs*): I can't believe the Jews actually crucified their Messiah.
CLEOPAS: It was because He said He was the Son of God.
SHETHAR: The charge was blasphemy, then?
CLEOPAS: Yes. But I believe He is—was—the Son of God. And there is still hope. Some women were at the tomb this morning and they say it was empty. They say—
SHETHAR: I know. I heard they saw a vision. It's all very confusing.
CLEOPAS: Yes! They say they saw a man who told them Christ was risen. But if He is risen, I haven't seen Him.
SHETHAR: Nor I. But perhaps we will. (*Pause.*) Perhaps we will.
CLEOPAS: You aren't from around here, are you?

The Wise Man and the Shepherd

SHETHAR: No. I'm from the East. Shethar is my name.

CLEOPAS: Glad to meet you. I'm Cleopas. But what brings you to Jerusalem?

SHETHAR: It's a long story. I came to see the Christ. I saw Him when I was just a child, you see, and—

CLEOPAS: When you were a child you saw Him? What were you doing in Jerusalem as a child?

SHETHAR: My father was a Magus. He knew the stars and the Scriptures well. *(Musing and nodding his head as if in regret.)* Better than I do. *(Sighs.)* Anyway, he learned that the Christ would be born in Bethlehem, so when He saw the new star in the night sky, he and my uncles and other Magi planned the trip here.

CLEOPAS: So you came with the Magi from the east to see Christ as a child in Bethlehem? What was that like?

SHETHAR: I was only ten years old at the time. I was more interested in the trip here than in seeing a king. We had a few sand storms that delayed us, and we had to stay and let the livestock graze for weeks at a time. It was a long and tedious trip, but at the same time, exciting for me. Each night, my father showed me that the star was still leading us westward to Bethlehem. And each night he would read to me from the Scriptures about how the Savior was to be born.

CLEOPAS: And when you got to Bethlehem, what was that like?

SHETHAR: Looking on His face? *(Looks up to the sky and sighs.)* I really can't explain it. I just knew, you know?

CLEOPAS: Yes. I know.

CHOIR: "O Come, All Ye Faithful" *(or your selection)*

VIDEO: Scene of wise men bowing to worship the Christ child.

SHETHAR: We brought gifts. Gold for a king; frankincense for worship; and myrrh for well—

CLEOPAS: Burial.

SHETHAR: For burial. But I don't think my father knew He would need the myrrh so soon. *(Shakes his head.)*

CLEOPAS: Quite a disappointment.

SHETHAR: Yes, to all of us. But what about you? How long have you known the Christ?

CLEOPAS: Well, this is going to surprise you, but I actually got to meet Jesus even before you did.

SHETHAR *(looking astonished)*: Tell me about it.

CLEOPAS: Well, my uncle is a shepherd. Keeps a flock on the hills just south of Bethlehem. When Mary and Joseph came to Bethlehem for the taxation, I was with the shepherds on the hillside. You've heard about the angel who announced Christ's birth to the shepherds and the angel hosts, haven't you?

SHETHAR *(gasping):* You were there?

CLEOPAS *(smiling):* In person. And scared to death.

SHETHAR: I can imagine!

CLEOPAS: No, you can't. *(Pause.)* You really can't possibly imagine how frightening it was for us. It was like *(Pause.)* I thought I was dying or something. *(Shakes his head and sighs.)* But then, when we got to the manger—and we ran all the way—He was there, looking like, well, you know—

SHETHAR: —a perfect little Jewish boy.

CLEOPAS *(chuckles):* He was just an infant when I saw Him. But, yes, perfect. He was sleeping so peacefully. His face was round and red and sweet. . . .

CHOIR: "Thou Didst Leave Thy Throne" *(or your selection)*

VIDEO: Scenes of shepherds worshiping newborn baby in a manger.

SHETHAR: So I guess you did see Jesus before I did!

CLEOPAS: I suppose. But we both saw Him when we were pretty young!

SHETHAR: Yes, we did. But I wasn't here to see all the wonderful things He did. Were there really that many miracles? Did you witness any of the healings?

CLEOPAS: Oh, yes. I was there when the man born blind was given his sight. You should have seen him dancing with joy!

SHETHAR: I believe it! Makes you thankful for two good eyes, doesn't it?

CLEOPAS: Sure does.

SHETHAR: What about Lazarus? Was he really dead?

CLEOPAS: I wasn't there to see it, but I've talked to his sisters and I believe them. He was dead, all right. He was in the grave four days, you know.

SHETHAR: No!

CLEOPAS *(nods his head):* Sure was. I tell you, no man could do the work Jesus did. And, just last week, the people worshiped Him as a new king! He came into town riding on a donkey, and people were throwing their cloaks down on the path and cheering! *(Wistfully.)* Children gathered branches off trees and threw them on the road. Everyone was singing and dancing. It was a joyful celebration.

OPTIONAL: As Adult Choir sings, children come in back of auditorium in costume of the period, holding palm branches, singing, skipping and generally celebrating. They continue to walk up and down the aisles as they sing with the Adult Choir, and at the end of "Blessed Is He," they place their palm branches on the floor in front of the stage and stand in rows (*on steps if available*) facing the audience. They sing, "King of Kings" without the Adult Choir (*Clapping as they sing.*) and then the Adult Choir joins them in singing "How Majestic Is Your Name." Children's Choir exits after singing.

ADULT CHOIR: "Blessed Is He Who Comes in the Name of the Lord," (*Greer, Word Publishing, as children act out Triumphal Entry*)

CHILDREN'S CHOIR: "King of Kings" (*ancient Hebrew Folk song, Sophie Conty and Naomi Batya, © Maranatha! Music.*)

ADULT AND CHILDREN'S CHOIR: "How Majestic Is Your Name," (*Michael W. Smith © 1981 Meadowgreen Music Co.*)

VIDEO: Scenes of Triumphal Entry or houselights on for Children's Choir performance, and no slides.

(*Children's Choir exits.*)

CLEOPAS (*continuing with thought*): It was a beautiful day—and so much has happened since then! (*Pause, sigh.*) If He really was the Christ, He should have risen by today.
SHETHAR (*shaking his head*): Well, maybe He did. You've heard about the women who saw the vision. Maybe that was He.
CLEOPAS: Yes, and the tomb is empty. (*Sighs.*) I don't know. I just don't understand it.

(*Jesus walks up and two men continue to walk and talk.*)

JESUS: What are you discussing together as you walk along?
CLEOPAS: Surely you have heard the terrible things that have happened in Jerusalem these last few days!
JESUS: What things?
CLEOPAS: About Jesus of Nazareth. He was a prophet, powerful in word and deed before God and all the people. The chief priests and our rulers handed Him over to be sentenced to death, and they crucified Him; but we had hoped that He was the one who was

going to redeem Israel. And what is more, it is the third day since all this took place. In addition, some of our women amazed us. They went to the tomb early this morning but didn't find His body. They came and told us that they had seen a vision of angels, who said He was alive. Then some of our companions went to the tomb and found it just as the women had said, but Him they did not see.

JESUS: How foolish you are, and how slow of heart to believe all that the prophets have spoken! Did not the Christ have to suffer these things and then enter His glory? *(The two men exchange astonished glances.)* Remember when Moses was called out of Egypt and the Lord God instructed the people to slaughter a lamb?

(More dialogue here fades out as Jesus begins to tell them about Moses and all the prophets. See Luke 24:27, 28, NIV. The three men continue to walk slowly offstage as the Choir sings.)

CHOIR: *(Your selection)*

Scene 2

From Luke 24:33-49. In a room in Jerusalem, eleven disciples gather around a table. Disciples all speaking at once, saying: "I don't understand it. Have you seen Him? But Mary said. Surely it was a vision. Probably angels," etc.

ONE DISCIPLE: But it's true! The Lord has risen and has appeared to Simon!

(Two men walk in.)

CLEOPAS: It's true! He is alive!

SHETHAR: He walked with us! And He talked with us!

CLEOPAS: He explained all about the prophecies concerning His death and resurrection.

SHETHAR: He's alive all right!

CLEOPAS AND SHETHAR *(together)*: We saw Him with our own eyes!

DISCIPLE: But how did you two know He was the Christ?

CLEOPAS AND SHETHAR *(together, excitedly)*: Well, we—

SHETHAR: You tell them, Cleopas.

CLEOPAS: All right. We were walking on the road to Emmaus and He was walking along—

SHETHAR *(interrupts)*: Right there with us!

CLEOPAS: Yes, right along with us, and —

SHETHAR *(interrupts again):* We didn't even know it was Jesus, yet He talked with us! It was just wonderful! You should have been there.

(Cleopas glares at Shethar.)

SHETHAR: Oh. Sorry. You tell it, Cleopas.

CLEOPAS: Well, we were walking along wondering why nothing had happened—because of the prophecy about raising the temple on the third day, and here it was the third day since Jesus' death and all, and suddenly this Man—

SHETHAR *(interrupts):* But we didn't know it was Christ yet.

CLEOPAS: Right. But we didn't know it was Christ. This Man came up and was just explaining everything—

SHETHAR: And our hearts were just burning within us while He talked with us on the road!

CLEOPAS: Right. We kind of knew it was Jesus, you see, but we weren't sure.

SHETHAR: And then the bread. Tell them about the bread, Cleopas!

CLEOPAS: I haven't got to that part yet.

SHETHAR: Sorry.

CLEOPAS: All right. So, He had been walking with us for a long time— it's seven miles to Emmaus, you know—and He had opened the Scriptures to us and explained everything that was on my heart—

SHETHAR: Both of our hearts.

CLEOPAS: Well, of course. And there we were in Emmaus but He acted like He was going to go farther—

SHETHAR: But we couldn't let Him do that!

CLEOPAS: No, we couldn't. Or we didn't want to. So we urged Him to stay with us—

SHETHAR: And He did!

CLEOPAS *(getting disgusted):* I was just going to say that!

SHETHAR: You go ahead, Cleopas. Don't let me interrupt.

CLEOPAS: And He did stay with us.

SHETHAR: Now tell them about the bread.

CLEOPAS *(sighs):* So when we were at the table getting ready to eat, He took the bread, gave thanks, broke it, and gave it to us! *(Pause, then, to Shethar, who is dabbing at his eyes.)* Well, aren't you going to add anything?

SHETHAR *(with a catch in his throat, waves him on and says):* Go ahead.

CLEOPAS *(smiling):* As soon as He gave us the bread, our eyes were opened and we recognized Him.

SHETHAR: His hands—His hands were—pierced, you see. (*Pause, as he looks at his own hands, then, slowly.*) It's because of the nails. The scars were still there. And we knew . . . we instantly knew it was the Christ, risen.

CLEOPAS (*thoughtfully*): Risen. (*Sighs.*) And then He disappeared.

DISCIPLE: And now here you are.

CLEOPAS AND SHETHAR: Yes, now we are—

(*All disciples are huddled around together, and now they draw back so that Jesus can be seen in their midst, as if He just appeared.*)

JESUS (*standing with arms outstretched with palms up so audience can see scars in His hands*): "Peace be with you" (Luke 24:36).

(*Disciples, Shethar and Cleopas freeze in kneeling or standing positions, frightened, but worshipful, gazing on Jesus as Choir sings.*)

CHOIR: "Hallelujah Chorus" (*or your selection*)

JESUS: Why are you troubled, and why do doubts rise in your minds? Look at my hands and my feet. It is I myself! Touch me and see; a ghost does not have flesh and bones, as you see I have. (*Shows them his hands and feet; disciples and two men are amazed and joyful.*) Do you have anything here to eat?

(*Disciples give Jesus a piece of broiled fish, and He eats it in front of them.*)

JESUS: This is what I told you while I was still with you. Everything must be fulfilled that is written about me in the Law of Moses, the Prophets and the Psalms. This is what is written: The Christ will suffer and rise from the dead on the third day, and repentance and forgiveness of sins will be preached in His name to all nations, beginning at Jerusalem. You are witnesses of these things. I am going to send you what my Father has promised; but stay in the city until you have been clothed with power from on high.

(*Disciples freeze in listening positions; Jesus continues to speak, silently, using hand motions, while choir sings final song.*)

CHOIR: (*Your selection*)

The Wise Man and the Shepherd

A New Feature

Iris Gray Dowling

Summary: Jinny needs a new dress for a school concert. Her mother can't afford it, but prays for wisdom. Jinny is pleased with Mom's new creation. A suggested fashion show is included.

Cast:
JINNY, the teen daughter
MOM, Jinny's mother
MARIAN, neighbor and Ashley's mother
ASHLEY, a neighbor's daughter
WOMEN for the fashion show

Costumes: Casual contemporary clothes for all and a light blue dress. If fashion show is used, the four dresses will be needed.

Setting: One scene continues in sewing room.

Props: Parts of quilts, patches, variety of fabric, chair, sewing machine, needles, thread, thimbles, sewing notions, light blue dress and other dresses, VCR, video tape, Bible, schoolbooks, and taped music.

Suggested Music: "'Tis So Sweet to Trust in Jesus"; "A Child of the King"; "Trusting Jesus"

At rise, Mother is sewing draperies. Jinny, looking sad, enters from SR.

MOM: Hi, Jinny.
JINNY *(sadly, puts books on table):* Hi, Mom.
MOM *(looks up):* What's wrong, Jinny?
JINNY: I need a new dress.
MOM: A new dress! What for?
JINNY: I've been chosen to sing in the first chorus.
MOM: That's great. I'm happy for you.
JINNY: That means I will need a light blue dress.
MOM: Maybe you can wear one of your other dresses with a nice belt or attractive piece of jewelry.

JINNY (*a little sarcastically*): Sure, Mom! When everybody else wears a new one. Anyway, I don't have a light blue dress.

MOM: Jinny, you know I can't afford a new dress at this time, what with Dad not working. You'll probably only wear it once. My sewing money helps pay for food and other necessities. I'm thankful for all these work orders right now.

JINNY: I know, Mom! I didn't ask you to get me a new dress. (*Pause, looks at order list on the table.*)

MOM: Sometimes, I think I can't sew another stitch. My fingers get so sore from the needle pricks. (*Pause as Mom holds fingers up. Jinny looks at Mom's fingers.*)

JINNY (*sympathetic*): I'm sorry, Mom. I'll tell my music teacher I can't be in the chorus.

MOM: No, Jinny. Not yet.

JINNY: Mom, I know you don't have the money.

MOM: Now, Jinny. Don't tell the teacher yet. Give me a day or so. I'll ask God to help me think of something.

JINNY: Okay, Mom. (*Picks up her books.*)

MOM: I know God always helps those who trust Him.

(*Knock is heard. Jinny answers the door.*)

JINNY (*opening the door*): Come on in. (*Pauses; Marian and Ashley enter from front SR. All exchange greetings.*) Want to go to my room, Ashley?

ASHLEY: Okay.

(*Jinny and Ashley exit back SL. Mom looks thoughtful and sad.*)

MARIAN (*leans over table*): Is something bothering you?

MOM (*sadly*): Jinny needs a new dress for the concert.

MARIAN: Oh, my. I thought it was worse than that! Ashley has to have one too.

MOM (*sadly*): With my husband out of work, we can't afford a new dress. Jinny will probably have to drop out. (*Puts pieces of material together nervously.*)

MARIAN: Last night Ashley and I went to a fashion show. I brought a video for you to see. (*Takes video tape out.*)

MOM: That would be the worse place for me to go. I couldn't buy any of those dresses.

MARIAN: Oh, I wouldn't buy a dress there. I just wanted to see the styles young girls are wearing right now.

MOM (*raises eyebrows*): You mean they let you do that?

MARIAN: Sure. People who sew get lots of ideas that way.

MOM (*holds up the patches she is sewing*): But I don't make dresses. I make draperies and chair covers.

MARIAN: You could try one, couldn't you?

MOM (*holds up some fabric*): I can't afford to experiment, with material being so expensive. Besides, I have so many orders to fill.

MARIAN: I know. This video may help you. I'll start it for you, then I have to go. (*Puts tape in; leaves right.*)

MOM: Thanks, Marian.

(*An additional scene may be added here. Place a divider down center stage. Mother watches the video on SL while audience watches the live fashion show on SR. You may use the descriptions of the dresses you decide to include. Jinny returns to the stage for the fashion show. If you don't include this scene, use recorded music as Mom rests head on hands and prays. Skip to notation: "Pick up here if fashion show is not included in program" and continue with the play.*)

(*Girl 1 enters SR, slowly turns around.*)

ANNOUNCER (*SR*): Welcome to the annual Fashion Show. First, we have a beautiful pink silk suit with a lace collar and rhinestone buttons.

MOM (*SL*): That sounds too fancy for this occasion. I think of silk more for weddings or parties.

JINNY: Yeah, Mom. That's not the right material for what we want, but it is pretty.

MOM: It sounds like a nice suit all right.

(*Girl 1 exits SR; Girl 2 enters SR; turns around.*)

ANNOUNCER (*SR*): Here is a peach tea-length satin dress with sweet-heart neck and pointed bodice. Black pearls and black earrings as accessories give a stunning look.

MOM (*SL*): Maybe we could make a new feature out of one of your older dresses using a new belt and accessories. That (*Points to video.*) reinforces my thoughts.

(*Girl 2 exits SR slowly; Girl 3 enters SR slowly.*)

ANNOUNCER (*SR*): The next creation is a knee-length dress made of a linen fabric—not too fancy. The embroidered collar and flowered sash really set it off.

MOM *(SL):* Interesting! I wonder if that dress is expensive.

JINNY: I guess they're all too expensive for us.

MOM: A lot of people buy with credit cards, but we can't do that either.

(Girl 3 turns slowly and exits SR; Girl 4 enters SR.)

ANNOUNCER *(SR):* The last dress is taffeta with a chiffon overskirt. The top is decorated with sparkling sequins on the bodice. Any young girl would want this dress for her special night. *(Girl 4 put hands to bodice; turns.)*

MOM *(SL):* I certainly can't afford that by next week.

JINNY: I'll say. That's a great party dress, but not right for the concert anyway. *(Girl 4 exits SR.)*

MOM: I didn't see any dresses like what you will need, but they really looked nice. I'll look at the rest of the video later. I need to get back to work. *(Turns tape off; soft music stops; Announcer exits SR.)*

JINNY: There's no need to worry. I know we'll find a dress. You told me God always provides for us. *(Exits.)*

(Pick up here if fashion show is not included in program.)

MOM: I just need to pray and trust God. *(Rests hands on head; prays.)* Dear Lord, Jinny needs a dress for her concert. I know You always provide our needs. Please help me think of some way to get a dress. Amen.

JINNY *(enters from SL):* Mom, are you all right?

MOM: Oh, yes, don't worry, Jinny. God will help me think of something.

JINNY: I bet I'm the only girl who can't afford a new dress.

MOM: That's not true. Remember Esther, in the Bible? She didn't even have a mother. God provided her with beautiful dresses so she could be chosen queen.

JINNY: Mom, I'm not going to be queen. I'm just going to sing in a program.

MOM: No, but you're already a princess. When you know Christ as Savior, you're an heir of God.

JINNY: I know, Mom. I almost forgot I'm rich in Christ.

MOM: God also sees you with special white garments.

(Pulls length of thread to thread the needle.)

JINNY: I know it's more important to have God's garment, but it won't work for the concert.

MOM: I realize that. But you'll be wearing God's garment forever.

JINNY: I'm not going to worry about a new dress anymore. I'll do my best for the Lord, whatever I wear.

MOM: I love you. *(Mom gets up and hugs Jinny.)* You're just the kind of daughter I wanted the Lord to give me.

JINNY: Thanks, Mom. I'll go see if I can find a suitable dress in my closet. *(Exits SL.)*

MOM *(pauses as she thinks)*: Oh, what about that blue dress in my closet I was saving for my next anniversary dinner? Maybe I can work on it.

(Transition music plays while Mom exits SR and returns with light blue dress. Mom sits at machine sewing the light blue dress. Music continues as Mom takes more stitches.)

MOM *(says to self)*: I think I'm finished. It looks pretty good. I hope Jinny likes it. *(Pauses; hears noise.)* Jinny, is that you? Come here a minute.

JINNY: What is it, Mom? *(Jinny enters from back SL with another dress in hand.)*

MOM: Your blue dress is ready. Come, try it on.

JINNY *(surprised)*: My dress! *(Pauses. Holds dress up to look at it.)* Where did you get this beautiful dress?

MOM: It's my secret, Jinny. Don't you want to try it on?

JINNY: Sure, Mom. It's awesome. *(Jinny takes dress back SL. Mother starts sewing draperies again as she sings a hymn to herself. See suggested hymn list.)*

JINNY *(returns wearing the dress)*: Mom, it fits perfectly. Where did you get it?

MOM: I'm glad you like it, Jinny.

JINNY: It's beautiful! It's just what I need. *(Hugs Mom.)*

MOM: I thought about how God makes new creatures out of sinful people like us, so with His help, why couldn't I make a new feature out of an old dress? So I went to work.

JINNY: Mom, you're a genius.

MOM: No, not a genius. Just a mother who trusted God for wisdom.

JINNY: And He came through again, didn't He?

MOM: Yes, I had to be reminded of that once again.

JINNY: You're the best mother a girl ever had. *(Pauses.)* I want to be just like you.

(They hug as they exit stage together. Music plays. Houselights on.)

My Father Cares

Iris Gray Dowling

Theme: Being falsely accused; anything is possible with God, our heavenly Father. God works for our good. Based on Romans 8:27-39.

Summary: Jason finds his problems are not too big for God. Like Joseph he can trust God to work for good.

Characters:
JASON, boy with a problem, age 10 to 14
CHARITY, Jason's sister, a year older
MOM
DAD

Setting: In the family room.

At rise, Father is reading, Mother is cleaning, Jason sits staring at the floor. Charity is trying to get her parents to help Jason.

CHARITY *(touches Mom):* Mom . . . Dad . . . what's wrong with Jason? He's so grumpy!
MOM: Did you ask him?
CHARITY: Yeah, he won't talk. He just grunts at me.
MOM: Okay, I'll see what I can do. *(Pauses to put cleaning tools down; puts arm around Jason.)* Jason, What's wrong?
JASON *(still staring at the floor):* Nothing!
MOM: I know something is wrong. Tell me . . .
JASON *(grouchy):* I don't want to talk about it.
MOM: Why not? It might help.
JASON: Nobody can help me.
CHARITY: We're your family, we will try. If we can't help, God can.
JASON: My teacher accused me of taking Ross's candy bar.
DAD: Why would he do that? You have never taken anything before.
MOM: And you don't fool around in class, do you?
JASON: No, I don't. He asked one tricky question and I gave the answer he expected.
MOM: Does he think his question is fool proof?

JASON: I guess . . . but a piece of candy wrapper was found in my book.

CHARITY: I'd say you do have a big problem.

MOM: Should we talk to Mr. Brock?

JASON (jiggly words): No . . . I'll try to handle it.

CHARITY: You can tell him about Joseph in the Bible who was accused of a sin he didn't commit.

JASON: Why would I do that?

CHARITY: Joseph was a faithful servant in Potiphar's house. The master's wife tried to get Joseph to sin with her, but he said, "No."

DAD: And she didn't like that. She told lies about Joseph.

CHARITY: He had no witnesses or friends in this strange land. He had no one to say he wasn't guilty.

DAD: And the Egyptians wouldn't believe a servant over a ruler's wife.

MOM: I'm sure Joseph felt alone when he was falsely accused. He didn't have anyone to talk to.

DAD: Remember, he was in Egypt because his brothers betrayed him.

CHARITY: He was put in prison for many years. His family that cared about him did not know he was in prison. They thought he was dead.

DAD: And remember, he didn't know God's future plans to save the family from starvation either.

CHARITY: Joseph didn't have a friend to pray for him, but he did have God as his friend.

MOM: So do we, even though we forget it sometimes.

DAD: Joseph knew God was his strength. No one could separate him from God.

CHARITY: Wow! Joseph was an unusual guy, wasn't he?

MOM: We might think he was mistreated by everyone, but he knew God was his heavenly Father and was with him and that all things would work out for God's glory.

JASON: I guess I'd better be thankful my problem isn't so big after all. And my father believes in me and my family cares about me.

MOM: If any problems are too big for us, they aren't too big for God.

DAD: You're right. God sees the end from the beginning. He takes good out of unfair things in our lives and uses them for His glory.

JASON: I can't see how God will make good out of my situation, but I'll leave that to Him.

DAD: Just like Joseph, we can't see the future, but by trusting God, He will make us conquerors.

JASON: How did God bless Joseph in prison?

DAD: Remember how God gave him the ability to interpret dreams. Pharaoh had to ask him to interpret his dreams. Finally, he was made a ruler in Egypt and God blessed him.

JASON: Then I'm sure I can trust my heavenly Father to work for me. Thanks Dad for being a loving father to me.

DAD: God is our friend. Sometimes unpleasant things happen as learning experiences to prepare us for a bigger job.

MOM: He wants us to pray for His help at times when we have problems.

JASON: Okay. I'll talk to God about this. And I'll ask Him to help me talk to Mr. Brock tomorrow.

MOM: We'll also pray that Mr. Brock will listen and understand.

CHARITY: Maybe God wants you to be a witness to Mr. Brock as Joseph was to the Egyptians.

DAD: That's a good point.

JASON *(looks happier):* I'll try. Thanks for understanding and praying for me. You're a great family.

(All leave stage.)